THE BEDFORD SERIES IN HISTORY AND CULTURE

A Brief Narrative of the Case and Tryal of John Peter Zenger, Printer of the *New-York Weekly Journal*

with Related Documents

Related Titles in
THE BEDFORD SERIES IN HISTORY AND CULTURE
Advisory Editors: Lynn Hunt, *University of California, Los Angeles*
David W. Blight, *Yale University*
Bonnie G. Smith, *Rutgers University*
Natalie Zemon Davis, *Princeton University*
Ernest R. May, *Harvard University*

THE BEDFORD SERIES IN HISTORY AND CULTURE

A Brief Narrative of the Case and Tryal of John Peter Zenger, Printer of the *New-York Weekly Journal*

with Related Documents

Edited with an Introduction by

Paul Finkelman

Albany Law School

BEDFORD / ST. MARTIN'S   Boston ◆ New York

To Stanley N. Katz, my mentor and friend, whose work on Zenger has led all of us to better understand the case

For Bedford/St. Martin's

Publisher for History: Mary V. Dougherty
Director of Development for History: Jane Knetzger
Executive Editor: William J. Lombardo
Senior Editor: Heidi L. Hood
Developmental Editor: Arthur Johnson
Editorial Assistant: Jennifer Jovin
Production Associate: Samuel Jones
Executive Marketing Manager: Jenna Bookin Barry
Project Management: Books By Design, Inc.
Index: Books By Design, Inc.
Text Design: Claire Seng-Niemoeller
Cover Design: Richard DiTomassi
Cover Photo: Image of Page 1 of the Original 1736 Edition of *A Brief Narrative of the Case and Tryal of John Peter Zenger.* Courtesy of the Sterling Memorial Library, Yale University.
Composition: Achorn International
Printing and Binding: RR Donnelley & Sons Company

President: Joan E. Feinberg
Editorial Director: Denise B. Wydra
Director of Marketing: Karen R. Soeltz
Director of Editing, Design, and Production: Marcia Cohen
Assistant Director of Editing, Design, and Production: Elise S. Kaiser
Manager, Publishing Services: Emily Berleth

Library of Congress Control Number: 2009935127

Manufactured in the United States of America.

4   3   2   1   0   9
f   e   d   c   b   a

For information, write: Bedford/St. Martin's, 75 Arlington Street, Boston, MA 02116 (617-399-4000)

ISBN-10: 0-312-47443-1
ISBN-13: 978-0-312-47443-0

Foreword

The Bedford Series in History and Culture is designed so that readers can study the past as historians do.

The historian's first task is finding the evidence. Documents, letters, memoirs, interviews, pictures, movies, novels, or poems can provide facts and clues. Then the historian questions and compares the sources. There is more to do than in a courtroom, for hearsay evidence is welcome, and the historian is usually looking for answers beyond act and motive. Different views of an event may be as important as a single verdict. How a story is told may yield as much information as what it says.

Along the way the historian seeks help from other historians and perhaps from specialists in other disciplines. Finally, it is time to write, to decide on an interpretation and how to arrange the evidence for readers.

Each book in this series contains an important historical document or group of documents, each document a witness from the past and open to interpretation in different ways. The documents are combined with some element of historical narrative—an introduction or a biographical essay, for example—that provides students with an analysis of the primary source material and important background information about the world in which it was produced.

Each book in the series focuses on a specific topic within a specific historical period. Each provides a basis for lively thought and discussion about several aspects of the topic and the historian's role. Each is short enough (and inexpensive enough) to be a reasonable one-week assignment in a college course. Whether as classroom or personal reading, each book in the series provides firsthand experience of the challenge — and fun — of discovering, recreating, and interpreting the past.

Lynn Hunt
David W. Blight
Bonnie G. Smith
Natalie Zemon Davis
Ernest R. May

Preface

In 1735 the royal governor of New York, William Cosby, arranged for the seditious libel prosecution of John Peter Zenger, an obscure printer in New York City. The charge against Zenger was based on articles that had appeared in his newspaper, the *New York Weekly Journal*. Despite the fact that Zenger had clearly violated the law of seditious libel— indeed, Zenger's attorney, Andrew Hamilton, boldly admitted in court that Zenger had published articles defaming the governor and other officials in the colony—the jury disregarded the instructions of the judge and acquitted Zenger.

Zenger's trial was a major turning point in the history of freedom of the press and American political development, and Zenger's book about the trial, reprinted here, was the most important book published in America prior to the Revolutionary War. Zenger's case became a significant political precedent for a free press, the right of the people to criticize the government, and the right of a jury to ignore the technical requirements of the law in order to protect a defendant from an overbearing government. Despite Zenger's acquittal, the case did not bring an end to the law of libel or serve as a legal precedent for changing the law in England or the colonies. But the trial did change the politics of libel in America. After Zenger's case, no printer was convicted of seditious libel by the crown, despite existing laws, and the American colonial press became much freer and much more willing to criticize royal governors, parliament, and eventually the king himself. After the case, most Americans assumed they had an expansive right to a free press, even if technically they did not. This greater freedom of expression played a major role in the buildup to the American Revolution as colonists voiced their dissatisfaction with British rule. Zenger's opposition to the royal governor thus became a stepping-stone to the Revolutionary War. Recalling the arbitrary nature of the prosecution, later in the eighteenth century Americans demanded and secured such due process protections as grand jury indictments, impartial trial juries, and the right to counsel in the Bill of Rights. Most important, Zenger's acquittal laid the groundwork for the evolution of the ideology of freedom of the press that Americans cherish today.

Shortly after the trial Zenger published *A Brief Narrative of the Case and Tryal of John Peter Zenger, Printer of the NEW-YORK WEEKLY JOURNAL*, which tells the story of Zenger's trial and of the political and legal maneuvering that preceded it. While written under Zenger's name, the book was actually the work of one of his original attorneys, James Alexander. The *Narrative* became the most widely read American political pamphlet in the four decades leading up to the Revolution. Printed in 1736, the book offers readers a rich political, legal, and social text for the early eighteenth century, touching on the ethnic politics of New York as well as the growing sense in the colonies that America was significantly different from England. The *Narrative* illustrates how Zenger's trial was tied to emerging notions of liberty in the colonial period and helps mark the transition from dependent British colonists to more independent Americans.

In addition to its significance as a text for studying colonial, legal, and constitutional history, the *Narrative* provides readers with a fabulous understanding of how the best lawyers, nearly three hundred years ago, used rhetoric, argument, sarcasm, and logic. Much of the *Narrative* consists of arguments made by Andrew Hamilton, who was considered the finest lawyer in the British colonies. His style of argument, his use of legal and nonlegal sources, and his logic are, in their own right, inspiring and entertaining. One has a sense that the Zenger trial was the best theater on Broadway in 1735.

While the *Narrative* has been reprinted many times, this edition represents the first time it has ever been published in an accessible format expressly for classroom use. The introduction in Part One places Zenger in the context of the politics of eighteenth-century New York and explains how the trial became an iconic symbol of the struggle for a free press that led to the Bill of Rights in the United States and to reformist legislation in England. It details the way in which Zenger's case became a significant part of the history of journalism, the history of freedom of speech, and the history of fair trials, and notes how the trial was referenced in times of crisis in the following centuries up through the Red Scare of the 1950s and beyond.

Part Two of this volume offers a uniquely accessible reprinting of the *Narrative*. Although Zenger's book did not have chapters or section breaks, I have taken the liberty of adding section titles and headnotes to guide students through the text. I also provide extensive footnotes to help students understand the key players in this legal drama, as well as to explain references that Zenger's contemporaries would have taken for granted but that are long forgotten by most Americans today. The related documents in Part Three provide several excerpts from the *New York Weekly Journal*, including portions of the articles for which Zenger was ultimately prosecuted; thus, readers can evaluate the nature of Zenger's paper and consider how its essays, satire, and stinging rhetoric threatened the autocratic governor of the colony. To provide a flavor of the opinions on the opposing side, I have also included a passage from an essay by a royalist from Barbados who criticized Hamilton's arguments and the jury's decision in the Zenger trial.

The appendixes provide study and research aids: The chronology highlights key events surrounding the Zenger case and its aftermath. The questions for consideration provide a starting point for thoughtful discussions and writing assignments. The selected bibliography lists works useful for exploring this case and its times.

ACKNOWLEDGMENTS

This book grows out of my teaching the *Narrative* in my American legal history course throughout my career. It is a better book, I think, because of the feedback I have had from students over the last three decades. This is now my third book for Bedford/St. Martin's, and as always, I have benefited from the terrific editorial process at the press. David Blight brought the idea of this book to Bedford, where I have worked with Katherine Kurzman, Mary Dougherty, and Heidi Hood in the development of the manuscript. I also owe a great debt to my editor Arthur Johnson for his incredible dedication, not only to the details of publishing but also to the scholarship and pedagogy. Arthur went beyond the call of duty to help shape this volume. In addition, a number of scholars—including Angelo Angelis of Hunter College, CUNY; Thomas Cox of Sam Houston State; Edgar McManus of Queens College, CUNY; Louis W. Potts of the University of Missouri, Kansas City; James Schmidt of Northern Illinois University; and Robert V. Wells of Union College—read the manuscript and pushed me to make changes that strengthened my arguments. Their comments illustrate the best in collegial reviews of scholarship.

The library staff at Albany Law School, and especially Robert Emery, was invaluable in helping me find a clean copy of the original narrative and of some of the other documents. As always, my administrative assistant, Fredd Brewer, helped in countless ways. In writing the introduction

I worked at the New-York Historical Society and the New York State Library. Without the staffs of both institutions I could not have written this book. I also owe a special thinks to Ellen Dunlap, the president of the American Antiquarian Society, who helped me find an original edition of Anglo-Americanus's response to the Zenger narrative.

I dedicate this book to Stanley N. Katz, my Ph.D. adviser and mentor. Stan's now out-of-print work remains the best edition for advanced scholarly study of Zenger's narrative. Under Stan's guidance I studied the development of freedom of speech. I first read the *Brief Narrative* in his class. I later wrote my dissertation under Stan, on the issues of slavery and law, but I always remained fascinated by the Zenger case. My dedication of this book to Stan reflects not only his mentoring but also his role as the nation's leading scholar of Zenger.

Paul Finkelman

A Note about the Text

Although the *Brief Narrative* was written in the first person, its primary author was John Peter Zenger's attorney and patron, James Alexander. While Zenger was in jail awaiting trial, Alexander helped publish the *New York Weekly Journal,* and much of the *Brief Narrative* was initially printed in that paper. At a preliminary hearing before Zenger's trial, Chief Justice James De Lancey disbarred Alexander. Zenger's friends, or most likely Alexander himself, then secured the services of the renowned Philadelphia lawyer Andrew Hamilton. After Alexander drafted the *Brief Narrative,* he sent it to Hamilton, who made some changes based on his notes of his arguments in the case. In September 1735, Zenger announced in his newspaper that the *Brief Narrative* was in production; he advertised it in the June 21, 1736, issue of the *Weekly Journal.*

Aside from the insertion of section headings and headnotes to guide students as they read, the text of the *Narrative* published here is virtually identical to the original 1736 version. I have corrected obvious typographical errors, including those Zenger listed as "Errata" at the end of the 1736 publication. In a few places, I have added words to the text. Those words appear in brackets. Footnotes reproduced from the original text are followed by "[Zenger]" and numbered in with my own footnotes to the text.

I have kept the original spelling as it appeared in the 1736 edition of the *Brief Narrative.* In early-eighteenth-century New York, spelling was often erratic. More important, the style was different from today. Some spelling differences from then to now simply reflect modern distinctions between British and American spelling. For example, to this day the British use *our* at the end of words in which Americans use *or.* Thus, we find *labour* instead of *labor* and *neighbour* instead of *neighbor.* Zenger often added a *k* to words ending in *c*—hence, *publick* and *topick.* Some spelling differences between then and now are less easily categorized or explained. Following is a list of words found in the *Narrative* and their modern American equivalents.

ZENGER'S SPELLING	MODERN SPELLING
acquital	acquittal
administred	administered
alledged	alleged
antient	ancient
any thing	anything
arrand	arrant
attornies	attorneys
barr	bar
carressing	caressing
Catholick	Catholic
chuse	choose
compleat	complete
complicately	complicatedly
conferrence	conference
defence	defense
denyed	denied
dependant	dependent
dispence	dispense
domestick	domestic
duely	duly
endeavoured	endeavored
enjoyned	enjoined
enormitys	enormities
entituled	entitled
entred	entered
entring	entering
exceellency	excellency
falshood	falsehood
falsly	falsely
favour	favor
feaver	fever
forgoe	forgo
Fryday	Friday
fulness	fullness

goal	jail
governour	governor
heretick	heretic
holden	held
incerted	inserted
inclosed	enclosed
intailed	entailed
it self	itself
joyn	join
labour	labor
libeller	libeler
libcllous	libelous
lookt	looked
lyable	liable
lybel	libel
lyde	lied
lye	lie
medling	meddling
mispending	misspending
Munday	Monday
Negroe	Negro
neighbour	neighbor
neighbourhood	ncighborhood
newe	new
news paper	newspaper
offence	offense
offences	offenses
pannel	panel
Pensilvania	Pennsylvania
perswade	persuade
Powel	Powell
prefered	preferred
publick	public
risque	risk
sallaries	salaries

ZENGER'S SPELLING	MODERN SPELLING
shew	show
shewn	shown
shortned	shortened
stoln	stolen
supream	supreme
surprizing	surprising
taylor	tailor
tendred	tendered
tollerated	tolerated
topicks	topics
tryal	trial
untill	until
vilainous	villainous
witt	wit
writt	writ

Contents

A Brief Narrative of the Case and Tryal of John Peter Zenger, Printer of the *New-York Weekly Journal*

with Related Documents

PART ONE

Introduction:
Politics, the Press, and the
Trial of John Peter Zenger

In 1735, a jury in New York City acquitted the printer John Peter Zenger of libeling the governor of the colony, Colonel William Cosby. Zenger had been arrested the year before for "printing and publishing several Seditious Libels" in his newspaper, the *New York Weekly Journal.* Although Zenger was unquestionably guilty of seditious libel as defined by English law, his patron, the attorney James Alexander, outlined a strategy in which he would argue that Zenger ought to be acquitted because what he had written about the governor was true. Before the trial began, however, Chief Justice James De Lancey disbarred Alexander for challenging the legality of Cosby's actions in firing Lewis Morris, De Lancey's predecessor as chief justice, and appointing De Lancey to replace him. At that point, Zenger's supporters brought in the most famous lawyer in the colonies, Andrew Hamilton of Philadelphia. Working from Alexander's strategic outline for the case, Hamilton argued to the jury that freedom of expression was essential to preserving liberty in the American colonies because the colonists had to be able to criticize corrupt governors imposed on them by the British government. Hamilton challenged the procedure of the times, successfully persuading the jurors to ignore the charge of the judge and to decide for themselves whether the publication was libelous. He asked the jury to reach a "general verdict" of guilty or innocent on the entire charge of publishing a seditious libel. A jury of New Yorkers accepted these arguments and

1

acquitted Zenger. The jurors reached this verdict in spite of the judge telling them that truth was not a legitimate defense to a charge of libel.

This trial of an obscure printer in a far-off corner of the British Empire had a remarkable impact on the subsequent history of freedom of speech and the press, the importance of grand juries to the criminal justice process, the right of an accused to a fair trial, and the right to an attorney. To put it another way, the Zenger case was a precursor of many of the central protections of the Bill of Rights. In the more than two and a half centuries since his trial, Zenger's case has remained relevant to American culture and has been remembered in American law and even English law. When English authors and publishers challenged their own government in the last half of the eighteenth century, they rediscovered the case of their American counterpart, Mr. Zenger. At the time of the Revolution, Americans recalled Zenger as a model for those who stood up to British rule. When Americans complained that the new Constitution lacked a bill of rights, they reminded their countrymen of Zenger. In the 1950s, when Americans saw anti-Communist zealotry as a threat to civil liberties, they once again trotted out the Zenger case. As recently as the 1990s, U.S. Supreme Court justices have used the experience of Zenger to bolster their opinions.[1]

The lasting impact of the Zenger case was made possible by *A Brief Narrative of the Case and Tryal of John Peter Zenger, Printer of the New-York Weekly Journal*, which Zenger published less than a year after his acquittal. This small book recounted the events of his famous trial. Reprinted in England and America throughout the rest of the century, the *Brief Narrative* became "the most famous publication issued in America" before the Revolution.[2] In the years "preceding the War for Independence, the patriots time and again cited the verdict" in the Zenger case "as justifying their own assaults on overweening authority."[3] Gouverneur Morris, an early advocate of independence and a key delegate to the Constitutional Convention in 1787, asserted that "the trial of Zenger in 1735 was the germ of American freedom—the morning star of that Liberty which subsequently revolutionized America."[4] Indeed, inspired in part by the memory of Zenger, the American colonists repeatedly challenged British authority in the press. Colonial newspapermen and pamphleteers attacked government officials and policies with a vigor unknown anywhere else in the British Empire. Well before hostilities broke out on the battlefield, American printers and essayists began their own war against colonial governors, Parliament, imperial bureaucrats, and eventually King George III.

Whenever they published attacks on the royal governors or on imperial policy, American colonists committed the crime of seditious libel. It was illegal in England and in the American colonies to publish anything that challenged, undermined, or even criticized the government. It was equally criminal to publish disparaging comments or unflattering or unfavorable news about government officials, even if the published information was true. Put simply, it was a crime to criticize the government in print, even if the criticisms were true. As William Blackstone, the most important British legal commentator of the age, would summarize libel law on the eve of the Revolution, "The provocation, and not the falsity, is the thing to be punished criminally."[5]

Despite the law as it existed on the books, American printers of the pre-Revolutionary period published attacks on the British government with impunity. They understood the political reality of America: Since the trial and acquittal of the New York printer John Peter Zenger in 1735, the Crown had never successfully prosecuted an American publisher for criticizing a royal official. Whatever the technical law in England, the political precedent created in America by the Zenger case had led to a remarkably free press. Thus, in 1770 a patriot leader in New York declared that seditious libel prosecutions had been rejected "in the form of ZENGER." When Britain repealed the Stamp Act, the New York Sons of Liberty drank toasts to "Zenger's jury" and to the "Memory of Andrew Hamilton, Esq.," the Philadelphia lawyer who had successfully defended Zenger.[6]

For more than two centuries after his trial, historians portrayed Zenger as a courageous colonial printer, challenging an arbitrary and tyrannical colonial governor and in the process changing the law of libel. This classic view of Zenger is not wholly accurate. The story is more complicated. Modern scholarship reveals that James Alexander and his political allies, rather than Zenger, actually wrote much of what Zenger published. A good deal of the rest came from English authors, as Zenger's paper became a "veritable anthology of the writings of John Trenchard and Thomas Gordon," the authors of *Cato's Letters*, as well as the writings of other English libertarian philosophers.[7] Thus, while the newspaper attacked the governor and defended freedom of the press, Zenger functioned mostly as a printer, not as an editor or a publisher in the modern sense of the terms.

Zenger's background certainly did not prepare him for the role of crusading editor. He came to New York in 1710 as a thirteen-year-old

German immigrant. For eight years, he was an apprentice to William Bradford, who in the 1730s was the publisher of the pro-Cosby *New York Gazette*. After his apprenticeship, the twenty-one-year-old Zenger moved to Philadelphia, where he married Mary White, and then went on to Maryland, where he hoped to become the official printer of the colony. By 1723, his Maryland venture had failed, Mary had died, and Zenger had returned to New York, where he married Anna Catharina Maulin and made his living printing small publications, often Dutch religious tracts. He formed a temporary partnership with Bradford, his former master, but by 1726 he was once again on his own. In 1730, he published the first arithmetic textbook in America; the following year he served briefly as a tax collector.[8]

Zenger appears to have agreed to print the *New York Weekly Journal* because he was paid to do so and because, as one observer at the time concluded, he was "unable to subsist by other printing work."[9] But despite his apparently nonpolitical motivation for printing the paper, we should not underestimate Zenger's political involvement. Even before he began publishing the *Weekly Journal*, Zenger was working with Lewis Morris, James Alexander, and their allies, publishing their pamphlets attacking Cosby.[10] By printing attacks on the royal governor, Zenger knew he was risking prosecution and jail. His willingness to escalate the attacks on Cosby by publishing the *Weekly Journal* suggests that he was neither politically naive nor uninvolved. While publishing the *Journal*, he also continued to publish new pamphlets attacking Cosby. Zenger also joined nearly three hundred other New Yorkers—many of them prominent politicians and wealthy landowners—in supporting Morris, who in 1735 went to London to protest Cosby's rule.[11] In the *Weekly Journal*, Morris and his allies launched an all-out attack on Cosby. Zenger, aware of the risks, occasionally showed restraint. In a few instances, he put dashes in an article, saying, "Something is here omitted . . . as it is not safe for me to print."[12] But generally Zenger seemed fearless in attacking Cosby. As historian Stanley N. Katz concluded, "On the whole the *Journal* was looking for trouble."[13] After his arrest, Zenger spent more than eight months in jail while awaiting trial. Not intending to be a martyr for a free press, Zenger knew the dangers that came with challenging the authority of Governor Cosby and violating the settled law of seditious libel. Presumably, he might have struck a deal with the prosecutor to turn on his patrons in exchange for leniency. Instead, he bravely endured jail and accepted the risks associated with Alexander's defense strategy.

Before the 1960s, historians argued that Zenger's trial "established freedom of the press in North America" and "wrought an important change in the law of libel."[14] Our understanding of the legal significance of Zenger's case has since evolved and changed. Historians now agree that the case did not have an immediate impact on libel law in either the American colonies or Great Britain. As late as the 1790s, English and American law continued to define as criminal any substantial criticism of the government, whether truthful or not. Zenger's case was not, then, a precedent that immediately changed the law.[15] This is not surprising. Most precedents come from judicial opinions interpreting the law. Zenger's acquittal resulted from the independent decision of the jury to ignore the judge's instructions. As a matter of technical legal history, Zenger's case was merely an instance of a colonial jury, far from the center of lawmaking in the British Empire, refusing to convict an editor who criticized an unpopular royal governor. Zenger's acquittal was what modern legal scholars call "jury nullification"—the jury refused to enforce the law because the jurors thought the prosecution unfair.

If Zenger's case did not change the law, why do we care about it? And why did Americans during the Revolutionary period care? The reason is simple enough. While not a legal precedent, Zenger's case became an important political precedent for a free press, the right of the people to criticize the government, and the right of a jury to ignore the technical requirements of the law in order to protect a defendant from an overbearing government. In America, the case inspired patriots during the Revolution, supporters of a bill of rights during the struggle for the ratification of the Constitution, and opponents of the Sedition Act of 1798. The arbitrary nature of the prosecution was remembered later in the eighteenth century as Americans demanded and secured such due process protections as grand jury indictments, impartial trial juries, and the right to counsel. The trial also inspired eighteenth-century British opponents of arbitrary government. Most important, Zenger's acquittal laid the groundwork for the evolution of the ideology of freedom of the press that Americans cherish today.

Since the Revolution, the memory of the brave printer and his struggle for a free press has helped shape the Constitution, the Bill of Rights, and the modern understanding of civil liberties. To understand the importance of Zenger and the *Brief Narrative*, we must start with the politics of New York in the 1730s. The story begins with the appointment of Colonel William Cosby as the royal governor of New York and New Jersey.

GOVERNOR WILLIAM COSBY
AND NEW YORK POLITICS

William Cosby was the tenth son of an Anglo-Irish family of gentlemanly status but without great assets.[16] He entered the army and had a thoroughly unspectacular career as a military officer and a minor cog in Britain's growing colonial bureaucracy. From 1718 to 1728, he was the governor of Minorca, a small island in the Mediterranean Sea off the coast of Spain, where he earned a reputation for being autocratic, greedy, and incompetent. In 1718, he illegally seized the goods of a Portuguese merchant, for which he later was forced to pay damages of £10,000, an enormous amount that left Cosby in desperate financial circumstances. Cosby needed a new position that would allow him to recoup his losses. The American colonies offered such a possibility.

Like many colonial officials, Colonel William Cosby gained his governorship not because of any special skill, but because of family connections. Despite his relatively poor background, Cosby married well. His wife, Grace Montagu, was the sister of the Earl of Halifax, a member of the king's Privy Council. His wife's first cousin, the Duke of Newcastle, was the secretary of state for the Southern Department, which included the American colonies.[17] In 1731, these powerful patrons secured Cosby's appointment as governor of the Leeward Islands in the eastern Caribbean. But just as he was leaving for his new post, Cosby found out that John Montgomerie, the governor of New York, had died. Cosby returned to London, lobbied his in-laws, and soon had the higher-paying and more prestigious position of governor of New York. This also made him the governor of New York's smaller neighbor, New Jersey.

The colony Cosby was asked to govern was a diverse and complicated place. The Dutch first settled the colony in the 1620s, calling it New Netherland, with its main city called New Amsterdam. In 1664, a British fleet sailed into New Amsterdam harbor and seized the Dutch colony, which by this time also included New Jersey and Delaware. By the time of Cosby's arrival, the Dutch and English were beginning to integrate, but the ethnic polyglot of New York created tensions, competition, and conflict. The colony had a substantial slave population, a significant number of French Protestants (Huguenots), a sizable Dutch population, and a growing English population. In the 1680s, Thomas Dongan, the royal governor of the colony, noted: "Here bee not many of the Church of England; [a] few Roman Catholicks; abundance of Quakers preachers men and women especially; Singing Quakers, Ranting Quakers; Sabbatarians; Antisabbatarians; Some Anabaptists; some Independents; some

Jews; in short of all opinions there are some, and the most part none at all."[18] This religious diversity mirrored the racial and ethnic diversity of the colony. In the 1730s, some twenty languages could be heard as Africans, Europeans, and Indians mingled in the streets of New York City. To Cosby, who had lived only in Europe and mostly in Britain, New York must have seemed strange, exotic, and perhaps a bit frightening. His sensitivity to criticism, which led to the Zenger trial, may have been exacerbated by anxieties caused by living in such a diverse colony with so many competing groups and internal tensions. But even without these tensions, Cosby would probably have urged Zenger's prosecution. A military man, haughty and egotistical, Cosby was not the kind of ruler to tolerate any criticism.

Cosby was appointed governor of New York in July 1731 but did not arrive in the colony until August 1, 1732. During this period, he unsuccessfully lobbied against pending legislation in England regulating the importation of sugar, which he believed would adversely affect New York's economic interests. While Cosby remained in England, Rip Van Dam, a prominent Anglo-Dutch politician and merchant, was the colony's acting governor. As such, he collected all of Cosby's salary, about £1,975 in New York currency. He had done this with the consent of every member of the New York Council[19] except James De Lancey, the youngest member of the council, who after years in England clearly saw himself as an ally of the Crown and thus opposed enriching Van Dam (who was also a rival for power in the colony) at the expense of the new royal governor. At the same time, however, more than £6,400 of other monies accumulated for Cosby, mostly from the sale of lands and fees the governor received for various services and actions. When Cosby arrived in New York, the legislature voted to guarantee his salary for five years.

Cosby quickly squandered this show of goodwill by his seemingly insatiable demands for money. He bullied the legislature into giving him a £1,000 bonus for his failed efforts in England to secure favorable trade regulations for New York. His demand for this bonus was a grotesque act of greed that angered many New Yorkers, and it directly violated Cosby's written instructions from the Board of Trade, which explicitly prohibited him from taking such "gifts" from the colonial legislature.[20] Nevertheless, he pestered the legislature for the money and happily pocketed it. Thus, shortly after his arrival, Cosby received about £7,400.[21]

Cosby did not stop with lining his own pockets and thus continued to offend local leaders and the general populace. He appointed his son, disrespectfully called "Billy" by the colonists, as the secretary of New

Jersey, taking that choice patronage plum away from local politicians. Soon after taking office, Cosby allegedly accepted payments or kickbacks for appointing people to various public offices. He persuaded the Mohawk Indians to burn a deed giving one thousand acres of land to the city of Albany, and he supported English land speculators in a dispute with colonists over a land claim. He held meetings of his council without notifying those members—including James Alexander, Lewis Morris, and Cadwallader Colden—who opposed his policies.[22] He was, from the beginning, officious, overbearing, and obnoxious.

Most important, Cosby aggressively sought to obtain even more money. At a meeting of the New York Council on November 14, Cosby demanded that Van Dam relinquish half the salary he had collected while he was acting governor. Cosby's official instructions from the government in London declared that he had a right to this money.[23] But by demanding this money at the council meeting, Cosby managed to offend Van Dam and other political leaders. Furthermore, the demand seemed excessively greedy, since the legislature had already given Cosby the questionable £1,000 bonus, which was slightly more than the £988 Cosby now sought from Van Dam. At the next meeting of the council, Van Dam formally refused to give up the money, claiming that he had earned it.

In addition to Van Dam wanting to keep money already in his hands, his refusal was clearly tied to politics. By this time, Cosby had alienated a number of New York politicians with his impolitic and high-handed behavior, and Van Dam had emerged as a leader of the opposition to the new governor. Cosby, still desperate to replenish his fortune, decided to sue Van Dam for half the salary he had collected. This set the stage for the crisis in New York politics that ultimately led to the publication of Zenger's newspaper.

Cosby could have sued Van Dam in a traditional common-law court, where a jury would hear evidence, evaluate testimony, and reach a conclusion based on the legal traditions of the community and of England. Common-law suits were usually based not on written law, such as an act of Parliament, but on the generally accepted rules of society.[24] In such a trial, Cosby's case would have been strong. The custom in New York had always been that acting governors took only half of the governor's salary. In addition, Cosby's instructions from the British government declared that he was entitled to the money. But Cosby did not bring his case against the "popular and reputable" Van Dam to a common-law court because "he dreaded . . . the verdict of a jury."[25] An outsider with almost no genuine support within the community, he stood little chance of winning his suit before a hostile New York jury.

The alternative to a common-law suit was a proceeding in a chancery court. Chancery courts decided cases without juries according to principles of equity, or fairness, rather than according to common-law rules. The governor of New York, however, was also the colony's chancellor, which made him the sole judge in all chancery court proceedings.[26] Even the politically inept and corrupt Cosby realized that he could not sit in judgment over his own lawsuit. At the suggestion of his lawyers, Daniel Horsmanden and Joseph Murray, Cosby asked his council to authorize the New York Supreme Court to sit as a court of exchequer.[27] Like chancery courts, exchequer courts operated according to the rules of equity, which meant that cases were decided without a jury and without following common-law rules, procedures, or precedents. Furthermore, equity courts had no witnesses, testimony, or cross-examination, but instead relied entirely on affidavits and legal arguments to determine the outcome of a case. In England, the Crown used the Exchequer Court to obtain monetary judgments for the failure to pay taxes or rents. Famously, in 1637 the Crown had brought John Hampden to the Court of the Exchequer Chamber when he refused to pay taxes that were not authorized by Parliament. Hampden's defiance made him a hero among those opposed to arbitrary government in England and America and helped precipitate the English Civil War.[28] Hampden's case made the Exchequer Court unpopular and appear to be an arm of arbitrary administrations. As a result, Cosby's request that New York import the juryless exchequer court undermined his already diminished popularity.

Equity jurisprudence liberated courts from the technicalities of the common law and the emotions of jurors, placing justice in the hands of appointed judges. In New York, landlords often used equity courts to collect rents, while powerful members of society turned to them to settle land disputes, usually against poorer and less influential claimants. Most New Yorkers who were familiar with the legal system wanted courts in which legal proceedings followed common-law rules and juries decided the issues.[29] Even the wealthy and aristocratic Lewis Morris, who was chief justice of the New York Supreme Court, disliked equity courts. He wanted Englishmen, including those in the province of New York, to be protected by "Judgment of their Peers . . . according to the good old Law."[30]

This opposition to equity courts probably originated in narrow controversies involving particular individuals who lost their land or money in chancery courts. But whatever motivated their original opposition, New Yorkers feared the arbitrary justice meted out by equity courts. In 1702, 1708, and 1727, the popularly elected New York Assembly had "passed resolutions condemning in the strongest terms the creation of such a court."[31] Thus, Cosby's proposal that the New York Supreme Court sit as an exchequer court smacked of tyranny because it was against the will of the people, as expressed through the assembly, and because he asked his own council to give the court of exchequer jurisdiction solely to hear his own case. At the same time, his refusal to sue before a jury of the community gave the whole transaction the appearance of corruption.

In February 1733, Cosby formally asked the New York Supreme Court to sit as a court of exchequer to hear his suit against Van Dam for half of the salary collected by Van Dam as acting governor. Van Dam then attempted to countersue for half the fees and other emoluments that had accumulated for Cosby while he was still in England. This sum far exceeded Cosby's actual salary. But the clerk of the court, a Cosby appointee, refused to affix his seal to the summons in Van Dam's case. Cosby then ignored the lawsuit, arguing that there had been no official service of process.[32] This was one of many instances in which court officials and Cosby appointees arbitrarily denied, or attempted to deny, due process to Zenger and others who opposed Cosby. Such actions led people to agree with the *Weekly Journal*'s subsequent claims that Cosby had corrupted justice in the colony.

Shortly after Cosby began his suit, but before the court convened, Chief Justice Morris conducted an exhaustive review of the New York judicial system and concluded that his court could not serve as an exchequer court.[33] On March 15, 1733, the New York Supreme Court heard Cosby's suit against Van Dam. Chief Justice Morris ordered the lawyers to argue just one point: whether the court had equity jurisdiction—that is, whether the court had the legal power to hear a case under the rules of equity. Chief Justice Morris's directive caught Attorney General Richard Bradley, who now represented the governor, off guard. Van Dam's attorneys, James Alexander and William Smith, were not surprised: Morris had warned them of his hostility toward the proceeding and sent them a draft of his opinion—written before he heard any arguments—on why his court lacked equity jurisdiction. As a result, Alexander and Smith came to court with a forty-four-page brief arguing against the court's jurisdiction.[34]

Immediately after hearing arguments from both sides, Morris read his opinion from the bench, denying that he had the power to hear the case and denying that the colony's supreme court could sit as an exchequer court. He found it "plain beyond the Power of Contradiction, *That there cannot be three Courts here, one of them with all the Powers of the Kings Bench, a second with all the Powers of the common Pleas, and a third with all the Powers of the Exchequer in England, all coexisting under the same Judges.*" After a long and extraordinarily detailed discussion of the history of New York's courts and the history of jurisdiction in England and the colony, he emphatically declared "*there never was, nor never was intended to be erected, any Court of Exchequer (considered as a Court of Equity) in this Province by any Act of Assembly, Letters of Patent or Ordinance* . . . and therefore no such Court existing."[35] Morris then adjourned the court before the astonished Bradley or the other two justices, James De Lancey and Frederick Philipse, could complain.

When Cosby asked Morris for an explanation of his ruling, Morris responded by hiring Zenger to publish his opinion as a pamphlet for the entire colony to read. This was an act that even a dullard like Cosby understood to be both a political attack and a personal affront. In his published opinion, Morris denied the power of the governor to ask the colony's supreme court to sit in equity and declared that the existing chancery court, over which the governor presided, was illegally constituted because it had been created by the governor and his appointed council rather than by the popularly elected colonial legislature.[36] Morris was on strong legal ground in making these points, but his highhanded manner and the publication of his opinion were also blatant affronts to Cosby. The new governor had challenged the political power of Morris, Van Dam, Alexander, and Smith. Morris's opinion signaled their counterattack.

Morris's action dovetailed with his ideological opposition to equity courts, but it was also motivated by political and personal considerations. Morris and Van Dam were political allies. Thus, Morris's decision in the case could be seen as narrowly partisan. Morris also had a financial interest in the outcome of the case. While Van Dam had served as acting governor of New York, Morris had been acting governor of New Jersey, which was also under Cosby's jurisdiction. In that capacity, Morris had collected some £632, and if Cosby won his suit against Van Dam, Cosby could also be expected to ask Morris to turn over half of his New Jersey salary, £316. This was not a lot of money for a man as wealthy as Morris, who owned more than eight thousand acres in New York and New Jersey and, with sixty-six slaves, was the largest slaveholder in the middle colonies. Nevertheless, "the chief justice was sufficiently exercised over the prospect of forfeiting such a sum to regard the governor's suit against Van Dam with misgivings from the start."[37]

Finally, Morris—who had served in various elected and appointed positions before becoming chief justice of the New York Supreme

Court in 1715 but whose political career had been in decline for some years—probably saw his dispute with Cosby as an opportunity to create a new political base. Morris correctly gauged the hostility of New Yorkers to both equity courts and the greedy and obnoxious Cosby, and his decision in the case was a shrewd political move. Cosby fully understood Morris's motives. He wrote the Duke of Newcastle that Morris "strikes at Courts of Equity to please the people of New York."[38]

In August, Cosby retaliated by unilaterally removing Morris as chief justice, a post Morris had held for almost eighteen years. Two days later, Cosby appointed James De Lancey to replace Morris. De Lancey, born into a wealthy and politically connected New York family, had been educated at Corpus Christi College, Cambridge, and then studied law at the Inner Temple in London before returning to New York. He had been admitted to the bar in 1725, become a member of the New York Assembly in 1729 (the same year he married the daughter of the mayor of New York City), and been appointed to the New York Supreme Court in 1731, at the age of twenty-eight.[39]

Following his dismissal, Morris organized a number of prominent New Yorkers into an anti-Cosby faction. Members of this group included Van Dam, Alexander, and Smith. Most of the anti-Cosby group had suffered under the governor and were being denied access to political power, land grants, and other economic boons.

These men "were neither political democrats nor radical legal reformers. They were, in fact, a somewhat narrow-minded political faction seeking immediate political gain rather than long-term governmental or legal reform."[40] Regardless of their motivation, the anti-Cosby opposition struck a responsive chord among New Yorkers. Cosby's imperious, arrogant, and greedy actions had offended not only important New York politicians but also many average New York voters as well. In 1733 and 1734, the Morrisites won sweeping victories in local elections, gaining control of the New York City government.

Morris's own election to the New York Assembly in 1733 illustrates the arbitrary nature of Cosby's regime. In October 1733, Morris ran in a special election to fill a recently vacated seat in the assembly. His opponent, William Forster, was a Cosby man with close ties to Justice Frederick Philipse, who also lived in Westchester County. Shortly before the election, Governor Cosby appointed Forster to the patronage position of county clerk, "no doubt hoping to give him some added luster with which to face his opponent, Lewis Morris."[41] The election had become a referendum on Cosby's administration.

As was common at the time, the candidates marched to the polling place with their supporters on election day. Each candidate tried to awe the opposition with a greater spectacle. Morris, who owned vast lands in Westchester County, arrived at the polling place with more than 300 mounted voters and other supporters marching under the banner LIBERTY AND LAW. Leading this procession were "two Trumpeters and 3 Violines." Zenger's paper later claimed this was "a greater Number than had ever appeared for one Man since the Settlement of that County."[42] Some time after this, Forster arrived with 170 supporters, led by Chief Justice De Lancey and Justice Philipse.

It was obvious to all present that Morris had the most votes, but Forster's supporters demanded an actual vote count. Moreover, the sheriff required that each voter "swear" to support the king. Because of their religious beliefs, Quakers refused to swear oaths. New York sheriffs usually allowed them to "affirm" their status. The sheriff, a Cosby appointee, refused to do this, thus disfranchising thirty-eight Quakers who had marched with Morris. This "violent attempt on the Liberties of the People," as Zenger reported it, did not change the outcome. Morris still won, with 231 votes to Forster's 151. The sheriff's actions simply underscored the complaint of Morris and his allies that Cosby was arbitrary and tyrannical.[43]

This election showed that New Yorkers who had nothing to gain personally by supporting the Morris faction and who cared little for the political or economic fortunes of Morris and Van Dam supported the right to criticize the government, and particularly to criticize the excessively obnoxious Cosby. Though formed for shallow political purposes, Morris's party soon transcended the narrow quarrel between Cosby and his opponents because the larger issue—the right to resist an arbitrary governor—resonated with the people of New York.

On November 5, 1733, a week after Morris won his seat in the assembly, Zenger began printing the *New York Weekly Journal*. The first issue carried a glowing account of the Morris victory, and for the next two years the *Weekly Journal* ridiculed Governor Cosby while presenting New Yorkers with a coherent and persuasive defense of the idea that newspapers should be free from political restraint by an appointed governor. Like the ideas articulated by the Morris faction, which proved to be bigger than the faction itself, Zenger's paper took on a life of its own. What began as a vehicle to attack Cosby evolved into an advocate for a free press and legitimate political opposition. Zenger continued to publish the *Journal* after Cosby was dead, and the ideology of the anti-Cosby faction, created through the paper and Zenger's trial, continued to influence New York and the other colonies long after Morris and his party had faded from memory.

JOHN PETER ZENGER, POLITICAL PRINTER

When John Peter Zenger began publishing the *New York Weekly Journal* in November 1733, he changed the nature of politics and print culture in the American colonies. His was the first opposition newspaper in American history. The paper was founded by Lewis Morris, Rip Van Dam, and James Alexander, a leading politician and the attorney who had represented Van Dam when Cosby sued him. Alexander had been the surveyor general in New Jersey and New York before becoming a lawyer. He served on the New York Council from 1721 to 1733 and was the attorney general for New Jersey from 1723 to 1727. Alexander's opposition to Cosby had already cost him his seat on the council, as well as access to various land claims.[44] Thus, Alexander, Morris, and Van Dam all had intertwined personal, political, and financial reasons for opposing Cosby.

Even before they began the *New York Weekly Journal*, Morris and Alexander had worked with Zenger to strike back at Cosby by hiring Zenger to print pamphlets attacking the governor and by challenging — and defeating — Cosby's supporters for seats in the colony's legislature and the New York City Council.[45] Flush from their victories in the 1733 elections, the anti-Cosby opposition hired Zenger to publish a newspaper to serve as a vehicle for their attack on Cosby. Zenger was the publisher of the *New York Weekly Journal*, and thus his name appeared in every issue, but the editorial work — the actual writing of the paper — was mostly done by Alexander, Morris, and William Smith, another attorney opposed to Cosby.

The goal of the *Weekly Journal* was self-consciously political. As Alexander told Robert Hunter, a former governor of New York, the paper was designed "Chiefly to Expose him [Cosby] & those ridiculous flatteries" that appeared in the only other paper in the colony, the pro-Cosby *New York Gazette*.[46] The *Weekly Journal* was humorous, satirical, and philosophical. It ridiculed Governor Cosby through innuendo and satire while at the same time printing high-level discourses on philosophy, political theory, and the lessons of history. The *Journal* also provided an articulate defense of the idea of a free press.

Of course, the paper carried political news, which almost always showed Cosby in a bad light. This was not hard to do. For example, in late 1733 Cosby allowed a French ship to dock in New York harbor and purchase supplies for the French fort at Louisbourg, on Cape Breton Island in Canada. This was potentially a serious breach of the security of the colony both because it allowed the French to take soundings of New York harbor and because England and France were on the verge of war in Europe.[47] The *Journal* did not directly attack Cosby for this breach of military security. Instead, Zenger published a series of questions that began with "Is it prudent in the French Governours not to suffer an Englishman to view their Fortifications, sound their Harbors, tarry in their Country to discover their Strength?"[48] (See Document 2.) The implication was clear: By allowing the French ship into the harbor, the governor had jeopardized the safety of the city. This was something a French governor would not do. The paper also pointed out that Cosby had violated various rules of his own governorship. Cosby had adjourned the assembly in his own name instead of in the name of the king, and he had demanded that assembly bills be sent to him before going to the council, which served as the upper chamber of the New York legislature.[49] (See Document 2.) Zenger's paper pointed out that these actions not only were illegal but also set the stage for arbitrary, tyrannical rule.

Shrewdly, the editors of the paper used more than traditional news to attack the governor. Some of the paper's most telling attacks came through "advertisements" and satires poking fun at the governor and his cronies. One issue contained an advertisement stating the following:

> A Large Spaneil, of about Five Foot Five Inches High, has lately stray'd from his Kennell with his Mouth full of fulsom Panegericks, and in his Ramble dropt them in the NEW-YORK-GAZETTE; when a puppy, he was marked thus **FH**, and a Cross in his Forehead, but the Mark being worn out, he has taken upon him in a heathenish Manner to abuse Mankind, by imposing a great many gross Falshoods upon them.

The advertisement declared, "Whoever will strip the said Panagericks of all their Fulsomness, and send the Beast back to his Kennell, shall have the Thanks of all honest Men, and all reasonable Charges."[50] New Yorkers easily recognized the spaniel marked "FH" as Francis Harison, the recorder of the city of New York, a member of the New York Council, and a Cosby crony who often wrote for the *Gazette*.[51]

The suggestion that Harison had been a good Christian but that his cross had worn off and made him "heathenish" illustrates the biting edge sometimes found in Zenger's paper. Less nasty, but equally effective in ridiculing Cosby, was the simple advertisement snuck in among legitimate announcements of ship arrivals that declared that a ship had arrived from "God knows where" with a "choice parcel of new authorities."[52]

Even more annoying to Cosby, no doubt, was an advertisement noting that "a Monkey of the larger Sort . . . has lately broke his chain and run into the country. . . . Having got a Warr Saddle, Pistols and Sword, this whimsical Creature fancied himself a general; and taking a Paper in his Paw he muttered over it, what the far greatest Part of the Company understood not; but others who thought themselves wiser pretended to understand Him."[53] New Yorkers readily understood that the "Monkey" with military equipment was Cosby, the former army colonel, who as governor was head of the New York militia. New Yorkers also recognized those who pretended to understand the "Monkey" as Cosby's supporters and allies.

Another issue of the newspaper contained an interview with a "magician" who pointed out the dangers of governors whose names began with "C." The "magician" declared that "C has always proved unhappy, either to the Government, or to themselves or both." Among others, he mentioned Governors Richard Coote[54] and Lord Cornbury[55] of New York and Governors Lord Neil Campbell[56] and Philip Carteret[57] of New Jersey, all of whom were notoriously incompetent, corrupt, or tyrannical. The innuendo was clear: Cosby, a "C" man, was simultaneously governor of both colonies. In case anyone missed this, the article ended with this reminder: "What has once been, may be again."[58]

The paper self-consciously declared that its purpose was to use the "lash of Satyr" on the "wicked Ministers" who ruled the colony.[59] Thus, an article noted that if "a Governor turns rogue" the people would find it was "prudent to keep in with him and join in the roguery; and that on the principle of self-preservation." The anonymous author compared previous governors, such as Coote and Cornbury, to the "very Bashwas as ever were sent out from Constantinople" and warned that "the dregs and scandals of human nature" would always appear to support every corrupt administration.[60] The reference to Constantinople here was particularly telling, because at this time Turkey was seen as the most repressive and undemocratic regime in the known world—the very embodiment of tyranny. Zenger even published "Aesop's Fable of the sick lion who invited guests in order to eat them at his leisure,"[61] letting New Yorkers draw an analogy between Cosby and the lion. On the more serious side, Zenger's paper introduced its readers to the Whig ideology of the early eighteenth century that preached the necessity of constitutional restraints on arbitrary rulers and the virtues of representative government. Finally, the paper offered a philosophical defense of freedom of the press, grounded in the paper's libertarian ideology. (See Document 1.) James Alexander and Lewis Morris wrote some of the articles defending a free press, as well as the direct attacks on Cosby's administration. But most of the philosophical and ideological pieces were reprinted essays by English writers such as Joseph Addison, Richard Steele, the great poet and essayist John Milton, and John Trenchard and Thomas Gordon. Trenchard and Gordon were the authors of *Cato's Letters*, a series of essays that extolled the value of a free press while attacking what Trenchard and Gordon considered to be the corruption of British politics, which they believed threatened English liberty.

The highly effective innuendos and satires reminded New Yorkers of the problems of Cosby's administration, while the essays on republican government and the danger of tyranny provided theoretical support for opposition to Cosby. Each discussion of Roman or medieval tyranny or reference to Turkish despotism drove home the point that New Yorkers might soon face the same problem. *Cato's Letters* never resonated in England because the radical Whig fear of tyranny seemed unrealistic to most Britons. There a petty and incompetent cipher like Cosby would never have been able to exercise significant power or authority. But in New York, the threat of arbitrary or tyrannical government rang true simply because Cosby did hold power. Thus, every mention of ancient or medieval tyranny or modern despotism implicitly attacked Cosby. The paper also offered a philosophical defense for the idea that the press ought to be free to print the truth, so that the people could learn about the evil doings of their government and protect their liberties. These theoretical arguments dovetailed with the needs of Morris and his allies: Only through a free press could political opposition function.

THE LAW OF SEDITIOUS LIBEL

Zenger's role at the *Weekly Journal* was essentially technical. A printer by trade, Zenger set the type and physically produced the newspaper, while Alexander, Morris, and Smith wrote most of the copy. Under English law, however, the printer of a publication was answerable for its contents. Simply by publishing the *Journal*, Zenger made himself vulnerable to prosecution for seditious libel.

In early-eighteenth-century England, a publication that defamed someone could be considered a libel. A publication that insulted an ordinary citizen was known as private libel. The wronged party could seek redress through a damage suit. Such suits were typically brought by wealthy and prominent men when their private lives and misdeeds were discussed in newspapers, pamphlets, and books. Although private libel could lead to a large monetary judgment, it was not criminal and could not lead to a jail sentence. Seditious libel was another matter. The author of a publication could be charged with seditious libel if the publication defamed the government or its officials or undermined the authority of the government. These English rules applied to New York because it was a British colony. The crime of seditious libel was punishable by fines, imprisonment, or both. The leading precedent, *De Libellis Famosis* (1606), declared that the danger of a libel on public officials was that "it concerns not only the breach of the peace, but also the scandal of government."[62] Seditious libel defied precise definition because the political nature of the crime made it subject to redefinition whenever an official felt threatened. Anything that might bring contempt on the government or ridicule to its officials or policies could be construed as seditious libel. In 1704, England's chief justice, John Holt, declared that seditious libel had to be prosecuted, because if publishers were able to encourage "the people [to have] an ill opinion of the government, no government can subsist. For it is very necessary for all governments that the people should have a good opinion of it."[63] Whether the offensive publication was true or false did not matter. As William Blackstone explained three decades after Zenger's acquittal, "The provocation, and not the falsity, is the thing to be punished criminally."[64] One English legal authority noted: "It is far from being a justification of a libel, that the contents thereof are true, . . . since the greater appearance there is of truth in any malicious invective, so much the more provoking it is."[65] Therefore, the maxim of English law was "the greater the truth" of an offensive publication, "the greater the libel."

The notion that truth made a libel worse was perfectly sensible within the context of English government. Readers were more likely to believe a "true" accusation than a false one. English judges understood that revealing the actual misdeeds of a political figure was far more likely to undermine his authority than telling a false tale.

In England, the jury in a seditious libel trial decided the factual question—whether the person charged with the crime had published the offending material. The outcome of the jury's deliberative process was known as a "special verdict." Judges reserved for themselves the legal question of whether the publication was actually libelous. This made a seditious libel prosecution different from virtually every other type of criminal trial in Anglo-American law. Because the nature of the crime had to do with the government and because judges rather than juries determined whether a crime against the government had actually been committed, both the offense and the trial were essentially political.

COSBY'S RESPONSE TO THE *WEEKLY JOURNAL*

Governor Cosby had little tolerance for the opposition paper. In January 1734, Chief Justice De Lancey, who was Cosby's man on the court, unsuccessfully urged a grand jury to indict Zenger for seditious libel.[66] In October, another grand jury agreed that certain issues of the *Weekly Journal* were indictable, but the jurors made no determination as to who had published them, even though Zenger's name was printed on the last page of each issue of the paper.[67] Again, there was no indictment.

Frustrated by the refusal of common citizens to indict Zenger, Cosby next asked the legislature to order the public burning of various issues of the *Weekly Journal*. The popularly elected assembly refused. Finally, on October 17, 1734, the New York Council asked the assembly to order that the most offensive issues, numbers 7, 47, 48, and 49 (see Document 2), be "burnt by the Hands of the common Hangman, as containing in them many Things derogatory of the Dignity of His Majesty's Government."[68] (Only nine of the twelve members of the council attended that meeting, for Cosby had refused to summon three members of the Morris faction—Rip Van Dam, James Alexander, and Abraham Van Horne.)[69] This was a shrewd attempt by the council to get the popularly elected colonial legislature to support the governor's attacks on Zenger. The attempt failed, however, when the assembly permanently tabled the request on October 22.[70]

On November 2, the council, with only eight members present, "ordered that the Sheriff for the City of *New-York*, do forthwith take and apprehend *John Peter Zenger*, for printing and publishing several Seditious Libels, dispersed throughout his Journals or News Papers, entitled *The New-York Weekly Journal, containing the freshest Advices, foreign and domestick*; as having in them many Things, tending to raise Factions and Tumults, among the People of this Province, inflaming their Minds with Contempt of His Majesty's Government, and greatly disturbing the Peace thereof, and upon his taking the said *John Peter Zenger, to commit him to the Prison or common Goal of the said City and County.*"[71] On November 6, the sheriff of New York asked the upper chamber of the New York City Council, which was called the Court of Quarter Sessions, to direct the common hangman to burn the offensive issues of the paper. The popularly elected and Morris-dominated

Quarter Sessions refused to do this.[72] Ultimately, the sheriff and a few other Cosby appointees publicly burned the papers. On November 17, the sheriff arrested Zenger under the order of the New York Council. Meanwhile, Attorney General Richard Bradley began preparing charges against Zenger.[73]

Only by employing arbitrary means could Cosby accomplish the burning of various issues of the paper and the arrest of Zenger. Two grand juries, symbols of "the people," had refused to indict the printer. Similarly, two popularly elected legislative bodies had refused to take any action against the *Weekly Journal*. By ignoring the institutions that traditionally protected the people from abusive government, Cosby was playing into the hands of his critics. His enemies had called him a tyrant; Cosby seemed bent on proving them correct.

After the sheriff arrested Zenger, he initially refused the printer "the use of Pen, Ink and Paper, and the Liberty of Speech with any Persons."[74] Once again, Cosby's men played their role as persecutors, denying Zenger his "rights" as most politically aware residents of the colony understood them. Whatever technical legal authority the sheriff had for holding Zenger under these circumstances, for most New Yorkers it smacked of the very kind of tyranny the *Journal* warned against. When a writ of habeas corpus[75] finally brought Zenger into a court, Chief Justice De Lancey predictably sustained the arrest. English law required that bail be granted "according to the quality of the prisoner, and the nature of the offense." Zenger was a poor man charged with a relatively minor crime, but De Lancey demanded £400 bail, ten times Zenger's net worth.[76] Because of this high bail and the strategy of his backers, Zenger languished in jail for nearly nine months.

The question of the stratospheric bail underscores the political nature of the contest for both the defendant and the government. De Lancey and Cosby doubtless wanted to keep Zenger in jail and away from his printshop, while at the same time making an example of him. Although Zenger could not make bail on his own, Alexander, Smith, or Van Dam could have bailed him out.[77] But if they had done so, they would have lost the propaganda advantages gained from his incarceration. Keeping a poor man in jail because he could not pay an outrageous bail was symptomatic of the arbitrary government the Morris faction claimed Cosby headed. Potential jurors would know of Zenger's situation, and that might make them more sympathetic to him. Similarly, the whole colony might be more supportive of the Morris faction when the citizens heard about one poor printer's plight.[78] Another reason for not bailing Zenger out was the belief that his stay in the jail would be a short one. Under English law, a prisoner not formally charged with a crime could be held in jail only as long as a grand jury sat. Once the grand jury ceased to sit, all unindicted prisoners had to be released.

The sheriff arrested Zenger in late November. In January, the grand jury would be dismissed, and since no one expected an indictment, Zenger's supporters assumed that his martyrdom would last only about two months. Six days after the arrest, Lewis Morris sailed to England to lobby against Governor Cosby.[79] He left Zenger's defense to Alexander and Smith, confident that within a short time, Zenger would be released from jail. Morris was certain that no grand jury would indict the printer.

Morris was right. The grand jury did in fact refuse to indict Zenger. However, Zenger's hopes for a speedy release "proved vain."[80] On the last day of the court term, the prosecutor charged Zenger by an "information."

An information resembled a grand jury indictment in most respects. But instead of resulting from the deliberations of a body of citizens, the charge emanated from the prosecuting attorney or some other government official.[81] Use of an information allowed the government to bring someone to trial at its own discretion. As a result, the system was open to two types of abuse. First, there was the potential for financial misuse of the procedure. A prosecuting attorney received a fee for each case he tried, so it was to his advantage to accuse people by information, even when there seemed little likelihood of a conviction. Early in his career, Attorney General Bradley was censured by the New York Assembly because he was in the habit of filing informations in order "to squeeze money" rather "than from any just cause."[82] Thus, among New Yorkers, the use of an information smacked of corruption. In 1727, the New York Assembly passed a law that prohibited charging people by information, but authorities in England disallowed this act.[83]

Second, in addition to creating the possibility for financial corruption, informations facilitated political persecution. If the administration disliked someone's political activities, an information could effectively remove that person from the scene, at least for the duration of the trial. Zenger's friends in the New York Assembly apparently thought that Cosby might use an information in his political war with them. Therefore, shortly after Zenger's arrest, the assembly considered a bill to make prosecution by information more difficult and to make the attorney general liable for all costs of the trial if the defendant was acquitted. The preamble to this bill declared that "people altogether Innocent have been prosecuted by Informations," that such people "have been fairly acquitted on Trial," and that "divers persons have been oppressed

injured and impoverished by such prosecutions." Attorney General
Bradley was sure that the governor and his council would not approve
this bill, but he nevertheless took time to tell officials in London that it
was pending. Bradley thought that these acquittals occurred because "it
is but too manifest that juries here very rarely find for the King tho' the
charge be never so well supported by evidence."[84]

Zenger's case illustrates the political use of an information. His
acquittal supported Bradley's complaint about New York juries, which,
he said, were likely to acquit those charged by information, especially
when they sensed the prosecutions were politically motivated.

For New Yorkers, the information filed against Zenger confirmed
the danger of Cosby's administration. Despite the narrow economic
and political goals that originally motivated Morris and his allies, their
appeal to higher principles worked. As the prime villain in a prototypical
political trial, Cosby played his part perfectly. Rebuffed by "the people"
in his attempts to silence Zenger, Cosby and his appointees ignored the
two classic representatives of liberty, the legislature and the grand jury,
and had the printer tried by information. Zenger's press had thereby
forced Governor Cosby to reveal himself plainly as a threat to liberty
and justice.

The substance of the information and the strategy behind it further
define the political nature of this trial. The information charged Zenger
with publishing articles critical of the government. What he actually
did—print a newspaper—became a crime only because the government disliked the contents of the paper. Murder, for example, would
be criminal even if it were motivated by political ideology. The criminal nature of the murder would not be determined by its political content. Zenger's act, however, was criminal because it was political. His
"crime," if removed from its political context, would not have been considered illegal. There was nothing inherently criminal about publishing
a newspaper.

Historian Leonard W. Levy argued that James Alexander, the mas-
termind of the *Weekly Journal*, and not Zenger, "should have been in
the prisoner's dock" because much of the invective against Cosby came
from Alexander's pen. In addition, Alexander also edited articles written
by others and acted as "the managing editor and chief editorial writer"
of the paper.[85] Levy's argument is well taken. So why wasn't Alexander,
the real editor—the real culprit—arrested?

Alexander "should have been in the prisoner's dock" only if we
assume that Cosby wanted to punish the individual most responsible for
writing the libels directed at him. But Cosby's motives were primarily
political rather than legal, and so Zenger was his target. Cosby wanted

to stop the opposition from attacking his administration. Jailing Alexander would not have accomplished that. Smith, Van Dam, Morris, or even the talented Cadwallader Colden[86] could easily have replaced Alexander as the *Weekly Journal*'s chief writer. Alexander might even have written essays while in jail, as "Freeborn" John Lilburne had done in England in the 1640s.[87] It is easy to imagine the scathing attacks Alexander could have directed at Cosby in his "letters from prison."

With Alexander in jail, the newspaper could still have been printed on Zenger's press. But who would publish the *Journal* with the printer in prison? And on what press would it be printed? While Zenger was in jail, Alexander published the *Journal* with the help of Zenger's sons.[88] But with Zenger convicted, it seems likely that members of the family would not have taken any more risks with their press or their liberty. A committed ally, such as Smith or Van Dam, might have risked prison to take Alexander's place as editor, but it is unlikely many printers would have jumped at the chance to replace Zenger and perhaps follow him to prison. Besides, in the 1730s there were few skilled printers in the colonies. In fact, Zenger and William Bradford were the only two printers in New York at the time.[89] Zenger was clearly the linchpin in the anti-Cosby newspaper. His arrest was one of the few shrewd political moves attempted by the Cosby administration. Had Zenger been successfully prosecuted, Cosby and his cronies would have dealt the opposition a telling blow.

Cosby also probably believed it would be easier to convict Zenger than Alexander. Zenger was a poor, virtually unknown German immigrant. Alexander was a talented, articulate, and wealthy politician of great prominence. It was easy to show Zenger's connection to the *Journal*, but direct evidence tying Alexander to the paper would have been difficult to obtain. Cosby may have thought that Zenger, once convicted, might be pressured into testifying against Alexander, Smith, and Morris.[90] Thus, for political and practical reasons, Zenger the printer, rather than Alexander the editor, wound up in the prisoner's dock. If Cosby secured Zenger's conviction, it would be easier to bring the rest of the Morris faction into court.

THE DISBARMENT OF ZENGER'S LAWYERS

On January 28, 1735, Attorney General Bradley formally charged Zenger with seditious libel for articles published in issues 13 and 23 of the *Weekly Journal*. (See Document 3.) However, Zenger's arraignment did not take place until April 1735. Thus, the defense strategy of not bailing him out at the beginning proved more costly than anyone anticipated at the time. Instead of spending only a short period in jail, Zenger had been incarcerated for five months by the time of his arraignment.

Alexander and Smith, two of the ablest attorneys in the colony, represented Zenger at the arraignment. In planning their strategy, they approached the case as a political trial; ultimately Zenger's defense would rest on political rather than legal arguments. Smith and Alexander began by challenging the right of Justices De Lancey and Philipse to hold their offices on the grounds that the judges' commissions were invalid. This complaint implied that Cosby and his justices were corrupt. In opening their defense by taking exceptions to the judges and the way they had obtained their offices, Smith and Alexander initiated a political attack on the governor and his administration. The trial would not be a defense of Zenger; it would be an attack on Cosby. If Smith and Alexander had their way, the courtroom would serve the same function as the *Weekly Journal*: It would become a forum for exposing the corruption of the Cosby administration.

The attack on the judges' commissions stemmed from the circumstances of De Lancey's appointment as chief justice. Cosby had removed Lewis Morris from that office without a proper investigation and without the approval of the New York Council, as required by law. (Indeed, the Lords of the Board of Trade in London would ultimately declare that Cosby had removed Morris illegally, although they would do nothing to return him to office.)[91] If Morris had been removed illegally, then his successor had been appointed illegally.

In addition to objecting to the manner of De Lancey's appointment, Smith and Alexander also objected to the content of his official commission. Zenger's lawyers complained that Cosby had appointed De Lancey to serve "*during Pleasure*," that is, as long as the executive wished him to remain, instead of "*during good Behaviour*."[92] This was contrary to both common practice and statutory law in England and America. The firing of Morris as chief justice and the appointment of De Lancey to replace him had every appearance of the worst sort of abuse of power, because it destroyed the independence of the judiciary. Lewis Morris wrote to officials in England, saying that Cosby "thinks himself above the restraint of any Rules but those of his own will." Morris pointed out that the people of New York would be unwilling to accept a legal system in which judges, "if they should not prove proper instruments for a Governor's purposes, may be soon removed." Morris argued that the "arbitrary removal of Judges . . . subjects the liberties and properties of the Inhabitants to the disposition of a Governor." Reflecting on the 1680s, when the actions of despotic English judges spurred the Glorious Revolution and the overthrow of King James II, Morris reminded his British correspondents that actions like Cosby's, which corrupted the judiciary, were "remembered with the utmost detestation" in England.[93]

In their challenge to the authority of the court, Zenger's lawyers also complained that De Lancey's commission conferred "the Jurisdiction and Authority of a Justice of the Court of Common Pleas" in England, along with that of a judge of the King's Bench. Smith and Alexander correctly protested that in England, one person could not simultaneously hold both offices.[94] Again, the threat to liberty through the concentration of power was apparent.

Smith and Alexander also complained that De Lancey's commission was "not founded on nor warranted by the Common Law, nor any statute of *England*, nor of *Great-Britain*, nor any Act of Assembly." Rather, Zenger's lawyers argued, De Lancey's commission directly violated English and New York law because Cosby had made the appointment unilaterally without consulting his council.[95]

Though respectfully drawn and presented, the exceptions to De Lancey's commission implied that Cosby's administration threatened liberty in the colony. The exceptions were not contemptuous of the office of chief justice but questioned the right of the present occupant to hold it. But while legal in form and content, the exceptions were clearly political in their thrust. The objections to De Lancey's commission challenged the authority of the governor and his justices.

De Lancey understood the political nature of the exceptions and warned Alexander and Smith "to consider the consequences of what they offered."[96] Ignoring this implied threat, Smith declared "that he was so well satisfied of *the Right of the Subject to take an Exception to the Commission of a Judge . . .* that he durst venture his Life upon *that Point.*" Fortunately for Smith, De Lancey had no life-and-death powers over the lawyers; he could control only the courts of the province of New York. The next day, De Lancey disbarred Smith and Alexander for "*having presumed*" to present the exceptions. This was a high-handed but shrewd action. Without Smith and Alexander, Zenger lacked sympathetic and skilled counsel. De Lancey's action confirmed once again the arbitrary and dangerous nature of the administration. The chief justice even prevented Alexander from offering motions on whether his disbarment was legal. Instead, De Lancey advised Alexander to "*get some Person to speak to that Point,*" because he was no longer allowed to practice law in New York.[97] This final ruling was also stunningly arbitrary. Under English law, a plaintiff or defendant could always represent himself, so even if Alexander could no longer practice law in the colony, he still should have been able to represent himself in any case.

De Lancey then appointed John Chambers to represent Zenger. Chambers was politically allied with Cosby, who had appointed him as recorder of the city, a valuable patronage position. Nevertheless, Chambers conducted a straightforward and conscientious defense. Chambers did not like Morris or his faction and probably had little use for Zenger, but as a good trial lawyer, he was committed to winning his case.[98]

Although he ultimately turned the case over to Andrew Hamilton, Chambers served Zenger well in the early stages of the trial. His first act was to prevent a stacked jury made up of Cosby's friends and supporters. Normally, juries were chosen from the "freeholders book," which contained the names of the colony's adult male property owners and voters. However, the court clerk, a Cosby appointee, offered a list of forty-eight potential jurors that was not drawn from the freeholders book. Many of these people were not even freeholders and thus were ineligible for jury service. Most of them were tied to Cosby, and some even worked for him. As Zenger later wrote in his *Narrative*, "my Friends told" the clerk that some of those on the list were "Persons holding Commissions and Offices at the Governour's Pleasure, that others were of the late displaced Magistrates of this City, who must be supposed to have Resentment against me, for what I had printed concerning them; that others were the Governour's Baker, Taylor, Shoemaker, Candlemaker, Joiner."[99] The clerk probably thought that Chambers would not object to the list because he was tied to Cosby's administration. But as a lawyer whose main goal was to win his case, Chambers understood that the key to victory was a sympathetic jury, or at least a fair one. Thus, he vigorously opposed this bogus list and prevented a stacked jury. Later, he also successfully protested when the sheriff altered the list of possible jurors.[100] Chambers's actions were critical to the success of Zenger's case. Ultimately, the jury consisted of a cross section of New York men, at least half of whom, far from being predisposed to support the prosecution, were in Zenger's camp from the beginning.[101] On August 4, 1735, Zenger's trial finally began.

THE TRIAL OF JOHN PETER ZENGER

When De Lancey disbarred Alexander and Smith in April, he scheduled the trial for August. In the intervening period, Alexander persuaded Andrew Hamilton of Philadelphia, the most famous and skillful attorney in the colonies, to represent Zenger. Hamilton had been involved in political disputes in Pennsylvania similar to the Morris-Cosby rivalry in New York, and like Morris and Alexander, Hamilton had opposed established authority.[102] As the trial commenced, Hamilton appeared without warning to serve as Zenger's counsel. In an age when a major trial like Zenger's was a form of public theater, as well as a forum for civic education, the surprise appearance of Hamilton thrilled those who came to watch the trial. His presence also startled and unnerved Attorney General Bradley and Chief Justice De Lancey. When Hamilton began his arguments, everyone in the courtroom was even more surprised.

James Alexander had planned most of Hamilton's presentation, which was both a wholesale attack on Cosby's administration and on the law of seditious libel itself. The defense argued four points. First, the allegedly libelous articles were true and accurate representations of the Cosby administration. Second, true articles could not be libelous. Third, the jury had the right to reach a general verdict of guilty or innocent and so determine both the facts of the case—whether Zenger had actually printed the newspaper—and the law of the case—whether the articles were in fact libelous. All these propositions were contrary to the settled law of England at this time. Hamilton in effect was arguing for a reformulation of English law as it applied to the colonies. This led to the fourth major point: Society and politics in America were so different from those in England that the law must also be different.

Hamilton's implementation of Alexander's strategy worked better than its proponents could have expected. Attorney General Bradley had planned to call numerous witnesses to prove the facts of publication—that Zenger had indeed printed the *Weekly Journal*. If the jury agreed with these facts, Bradley would have asked the jury to find a special verdict declaring Zenger guilty of printing the papers. This special verdict would then go to the judge to determine whether the content of Zenger's papers actually violated the law. With De Lancey on the bench, the verdict was a foregone conclusion.

Hamilton preempted Bradley's case by admitting that Zenger had published the papers: "I cannot think it proper for me (without doing Violence to my own Principles) to deny the Publication of a Complaint, which I think is the Right of every free-born Subject to make, when the Matters so published can be supported with Truth." Hamilton having admitted publication, the prosecutor dismissed all his witnesses. Bradley then demanded that the case go directly to the jury, which would have to find Zenger guilty of publishing the newspapers. Hamilton, however, interrupted by declaring that the attorney general still needed to prove the papers libelous. The information accused Zenger of publishing *"a certain false, malicious, and seditious scandalous Libel,"* and Hamilton wanted the prosecution to prove all aspects of the charge.[103]

What followed was hardly a normal trial. Hamilton offered to prove that in past cases, truth had been an acceptable defense to a libel prosecution. Bradley countered with other precedents holding the opposite. Although the law was generally with Bradley, he was unprepared for Hamilton's defense and so was at an extreme disadvantage. Hamilton, with Alexander's brief in hand, had come prepared for precisely these arguments. Furthermore, the experienced and skilled Hamilton was more than a match for Bradley and De Lancey combined.

Bradley argued that in England, a libel was dangerous because it would undermine the government and could lead to a revolution or civil war. Hamilton responded that this could not result from Zenger's paper because the real government was in England. On the contrary, Hamilton argued, only through an active press could the people be protected from corrupt governors, who were so far away from England that they could not be controlled by the Crown and Parliament.

Bradley contended one could not prove something was false, because "how can we prove a Negative?" Hamilton responded that an accused murderer might prove the negative by showing the "dead" man was actually alive.[104] Hamilton then magnanimously offered to prove the truth of each item in Zenger's papers and thus relieve the prosecution of the burden of proving a negative.[105] De Lancey refused to allow this, as it would have led to a wholesale attack on Cosby. Hamilton responded with a learned defense of his proposition, citing many cases that *"the Court had . . . under Consideration, a considerable Time, and every one was silent."* But De Lancey persisted in denying Hamilton the right to prove the truth of the articles.[106]

De Lancey based his ruling on the declaration in William Hawkins's *Pleas of the Crown* that *"it is far from being a Justification of a Libel, that the Contents thereof are true, . . . since the greater Appearance there is of Truth in any malicious Invective, so much the more provoking it is."* Here Hamilton responded that "these are Star Chamber Cases, and I was in hopes, that Practice had been dead with the Court."[107] De Lancey warned Hamilton to watch his manners and not to disagree with the judge. By pointing out that these were "Star Chamber Cases," Hamilton was obliquely implying that De Lancey was acting like a tyrant, in the way that Star Chamber judges had acted before the English Civil War. This comparison was mostly true—De Lancey was arbitrary and oppressive—but to make the comparison was surely dangerous. Clearly, De Lancey did not like being compared to a Star Chamber judge, and he nearly disbarred Hamilton for the insult. He probably did not do so because Hamilton was the most famous lawyer in the colonies, and the young and inexperienced De Lancey did not dare disbar him or hold him in contempt. Ironically, De Lancey's refusal to hear Hamilton's arguments on this issue underscored how arbitrary and unfair—how like a Star Chamber judge—De Lancey was.

Defeated on this issue, Hamilton turned directly to the jurors, asking them to use their best judgment as "Citizens of *New-York*," as "*honest and lawful Men*" who were "summoned, *out of the Neighbourhood where the Fact is alledged to be committed*; and the Reason of your being taken out of the Neighbourhood is, *because you are supposed to have the best Knowledge of the Fact that is to be tried*." He declared that to satisfy the indictment, the libelous matter had to be "*false, scandalous and seditious*." The jury knew this was not proved, he said, because the facts outlined in Zenger's paper were "notoriously known to be true." The "safety" of Zenger, and by implication the safety and liberty of all New Yorkers, rested with the jury.[108]

Hamilton succeeded in baiting Bradley into more debate. Each time Hamilton talked, he drove home to the jurors the point that what Zenger had printed was true. He discussed historical cases involving usurpations of power in England and the necessity of exposing tyranny. Without naming Cosby, Hamilton drew analogies between the corrupt and venal governor of New York and evil historical figures. These historical figures included King Charles I, who had been executed for treason during the English Civil War; King James II, who had been chased from England in the Glorious Revolution; and the judges, including those on the Court of Star Chamber, who had done those rulers' bidding. Hamilton also devoted some discussion to the notoriously oppressive Governor Francis Nicholson of Virginia, who had been recalled by royal authorities after he had personally beaten up a minister he did not like and then had the minister prosecuted when he complained about the beating. Hamilton ended this long soliloquy by reminding the jurors of Caesar's usurpations of power in ancient Rome.

Part of Hamilton's defense was based on the assertion that the paper rarely named Cosby. However, Bradley argued that Zenger's paper libeled Cosby not directly but through innuendo. Hamilton countered that by creative interpretation, a skilled prosecutor could make any publication into a libel by alleging that the libel was made by innuendo. To drive this point home, Hamilton turned to the Bible, quoting from the book of Isaiah:

The Leaders of the People cause them to err, and they that are led by them are destroyed. But should Mr. Attorney go about to make this a Libel, he would read it thus; *The Leaders of the People* [*innuendo,* the Governour and Council of *New-York*] *cause them* [*innuendo,* the People of this Province] *to err, and they* [the People of this Province meaning] *that are led by them* [the Governour and Council meaning] *are destroyed* [*innuendo,* are deceived into the Loss of their Liberty] which is the worst Kind of Destruction.[109]

Hamilton then quoted a second passage from Isaiah—*"His Watchmen are all blind, they are ignorant, &c. Yea, they are greedy dogs, that can never have enough"*—to illustrate how innocent language could be criminalized by an imaginative prosecutor. Hamilton argued that if the attorney general could bring an information against anyone who said something that could be construed as a libel, no one was secure.[110] Once again, the defense made its point to the jury about the dangers of libel prosecutions and at the same time managed, through innuendo, to attack the Cosby administration.

Hamilton's argument ranged from law to history to politics to a discussion of the differences between America and Britain. In closing, Attorney General Bradley observed that *"Mr. Hamilton had gone very much out of the Way, and had made himself and the People very merry."*[111] But Bradley asserted that *"all that the Jury had to consider of was Mr. Zenger's Printing and Publishing two scandalous Libels."* Bradley thought the jury should convict Zenger because he had already admitted that he had published the offensive material. Chief Justice De Lancey agreed, and he charged the jury to find a special verdict of guilty on the issue of publishing the papers and to leave the question of the law "to the Court."[112]

But Hamilton had swayed the jurors. They quickly returned a general verdict of not guilty. The court would not be able to determine the law in this case because the jury had acquitted the defendant. That night, the anti-Cosby faction held a great victory party, and the next day the sheriff released Zenger from jail. New York City later made Hamilton an honorary citizen, giving him an inscribed gold box and a certificate. Cosby died in 1736, and the Morris faction vanished. Zenger prospered, becoming the colony's official printer in 1737. He also continued to print the *Weekly Journal* until his death in 1746. Zenger's widow and her stepson, John Zenger Jr., ran the paper until 1748, and then John continued the paper until 1751.[113]

A POLITICAL PRECEDENT

Andrew Hamilton won his case because a jury of New Yorkers asserted the right to decide the entire case—both the facts and the law—and accepted the argument that a truthful statement could not be a libel. However, Zenger's case did not become a precedent for an immediate alteration of the law of seditious libel. The outcome was not, after all, in the form of a carefully thought-out and learned opinion written by a great jurist. On the contrary, it was the product of a single-minded jury, determined to acquit a man whose only crime was exposing the venality of an excessively corrupt governor. Zenger's verdict is a classic example of jury nullification—a verdict of innocent contrary to both settled law and the facts as they applied to that law. As Leonard W. Levy notes, "A jury's verdict does not alter law."[114] Levy argues that Zenger's was purely a personal victory, "like the stagecoach ticket inscribed 'Good for this day only.'"[115]

Although this case did not set a new legal precedent, it clearly set an important political one. Andrew Hamilton discussed the law as he believed it ought to be, under the conditions of colonial America, rather than the law as it was in England. His argument made sense to Americans. Things were simply different in America. A static, unchanging law was inappropriate for the colonies. Early in his argument, Hamilton noted it was "surprizing to see a Subject, upon his receiving a Commission from the King to be a Governor of a Colony in *America*, immediately imagining himself to be vested with all the Prerogatives belonging to the sacred Person of his Prince."[116] Obviously, the governor of the province of New York was not the same as the king of England. Hamilton then reminded the jury and the court "that if any Man strikes another in *Westminster Hall*, while the Judges are sitting, he shall lose his Right Hand, and forfeit his Land and Goods."[117] But no New Yorker would imagine that a fistfight, or even a melee in the New York courts, would deserve such punishment. The reason was clear: A riot in Westminster might lead to violence against the king himself, but a riot in New York could not affect the royal government. Later in his argument, Hamilton circled back to the fundamental differences between the colonies and England on a more mundane level. He cleverly pointed out these differences by comparing the rules on fencing land. In England, landowners were not obligated to fence their land. Rather, owners of animals were obligated to prevent their cattle, horses, or sheep from wandering onto a neighbor's land. In America, however, the general rule was that landowners were obligated to fence out animals and other trespassers.[118] This example, like that of the fistfight in Westminster, helped drive home the point that the circumstances of America called for new legal rules. The implication, which the jury readily understood, was that the political climate of the colonies also required new law. It was the political argument that carried the day and a political precedent that emerged from it.

One measure of the significance of this proceeding is the controversy it caused in the Anglo-American world. Judging from the volume of printed material concerning the Zenger case, we must conclude that eighteenth-century English and American lawyers and political thinkers believed it was important. In 1736, James Alexander wrote and Zenger published *A Brief Narrative of the Case and Tryal of John Peter Zenger, Printer of the* New-York Weekly Journal. Although the *Narrative* was written in the first person from Zenger's perspective, Alexander, not Zenger, was the book's primary author; in effect, he served as Zenger's ghostwriter. The book contained the substance of Andrew Hamilton's arguments and was probably in many places a word-for-word rendition of the trial. It also contained the arguments of Attorney General Bradley and the statements and rulings of Chief Justice De Lancey.

In 1737, two long letters published in the *Barbados Gazette* attacked Alexander and the concept of truth as a defense in libel cases. One, signed "Anglo-Americanus," was most likely written by Jonathan Blenman, the king's attorney in Barbados. (See Document 4.) Blenman restated contemporary English libel law in a carefully argued, well-organized essay filled with citations to cases and statutes.[119] "Indus Britannicus," the anonymous author of the other letter, lacked Blenman's skill and erudition but made similar arguments.

Alexander responded to these attacks with four articles in Benjamin Franklin's *Pennsylvania Gazette*. Franklin's paper was a logical place for this response. Like Zenger's paper, Franklin's was independent and not tied to the colony's government. The establishment organ in Philadelphia at this time was published by Andrew Bradford, the son of William Bradford, who had been the publisher of the organ of the Cosby administration, the *New York Gazette* (and who, like his son, had published a pamphlet in 1737 reprinting the Barbados essays).[120]

Alexander's response to the Barbados letters was an attempt "to support Hamilton's defense of Zenger by reference to history and law." But while "Alexander's essay makes a spirited espousal of the freedom of the press," according to Stanley N. Katz, it "does not come to grips with the basic [legal] issues raised by his antagonist."[121] There are two reasons for this. The legal precedents cited by Anglo-Americanus were much stronger than any Alexander could find to support his position. Alexander declined to debate Anglo-Americanus on strictly legal grounds because he could not win the debate on those grounds. In essence, Alexander's goal was fundamentally to change the law of libel, not merely to find an exception to the law that would justify the jury's verdict in Zenger's case.

Also, Alexander was shrewd enough to realize that his strength lay in the political and historical versatility of his arguments, not in the technicalities of the law. Although Anglo-Americanus made excellent legal arguments, Alexander made the compelling political point that "THE FREEDOM OF SPEECH is a principal pillar in a free government: when this support is taken away the constitution is dissolved, and tyranny is erected on its ruins." He supported this with references to Roman history and a recapitulation of the excesses committed by the Stuart kings and their judges. While not based on "good law," Alexander's argument was framed on a solid political sense and a useful application of history to the political world around him.[122]

In 1738, a London publisher reprinted the articles by Anglo-Americanus and Indus Britannicus under the title *Remarks on the Trial of John-Peter Zenger.*[123] This was undoubtedly a response to the appearance of the *Brief Narrative* in London that year. But unlike the single printing in England of the *Remarks*, there were multiple printings of the *Brief Narrative*. The London printer J. Wilford published four separate editions of the *Narrative* in 1738, while an undated one was probably published in 1738 or 1739. Wilford reprinted the *Narrative* again in 1750. Subsequent English editions appeared in 1752, 1765, and 1784. In addition to reprints of the *Brief Narrative*, English magazines and newspapers discussed the case and reprinted some of Andrew Hamilton's arguments defending the jury's verdict.[124]

Americans as well as Englishmen readily saw the importance of the case and the *Brief Narrative*. Just two years after Zenger published his *Narrative* in New York, Thomas Fleet reprinted it in a 1738 Boston edition, noting that reprints of the *Brief Narrative* in England had been met with "great Noise" and "*extraordinary Applause.*" Other American editions followed in 1756, 1770, and 1799.[125] Thus, in the years before and immediately after the Revolution, Americans read the *Brief Narrative* and recalled its lessons.

The many reprintings of this work suggest that Zenger's trial had a lasting impact on the development of the idea of a free press in both England and America, even if it did not bring an immediate change in the law of seditious libel. The context of the reprintings, and the various epigrams and dedications connected to them, support this analysis. The five editions printed by Wilford all contain the Ciceronian epigram "Ita CIUIQUE eveniat, ut de REPUBLICA meruit" [Thus as it happened to someone, so the country was served]. The 1765 London edition, printed by John Almon, also contains an account of the 1752 trial of William Owen, an English bookseller "also Charged with the Publication of a LIBEL against the GOVERNMENT; of which he was honorably acquitted by a Jury of Free-born Englishmen." Like Zenger's, that case was a victory for freedom of expression. The 1765 reprinting appeared when the controversy over the sedition trial of John Wilkes was still a critical issue in England. Five years later, Almon himself would be convicted for libel after he reprinted and sold the anonymous "Junius" letter, which "blamed [King] George III for a series of stupid blunders, advised a change in policy, and demanded a new ministry." The audacious Junius went so far as to remind readers—and implicitly the king himself—of the fate of the Stuart monarchs, Charles I and James II, the first of whom had been executed and the second overthrown and sent into exile.[126]

English radicals such as Owen, Wilkes, and Almon clearly saw Zenger's case as a political precedent for their own seditious libel cases. After Almon's conviction in 1770, London juries "stunningly returned general verdicts of not guilty" in the trials of five other printers charged with publishing the Junius letter. These cases and verdicts were reminiscent of Zenger's trial.[127] The right of a jury to determine both law and fact technically had not yet been incorporated into the law of libel. Yet a jury applied the Zenger precedent before no less a jurist than Lord Chief Justice Mansfield. Parliament debated the legal issues, while the British government dropped pending prosecutions of other publishers.[128]

In 1784, a London edition of the *Brief Narrative* was "Inscribed to the Honorable T. Erskine," the British attorney and advocate of free speech. The prefatory statement declared: "God and Reason made the law, and have placed Conscience within you to determine, not like an Asiatic Cadi, according to the Ebbs and Flows of his own Passions, but like a British Judge, in this Land of Liberty and good Sense, who makes no new Law, faithfully declares that Law which he knows already written."[129] Thomas Erskine believed that "every man, not intending to mislead, but seeking to enlighten others with what his own reason and conscience, however erroneously, have dictated to him as truth, may address himself to the universal reason of the whole nation, either on subjects of government in general, or upon that of our own particular country."[130] A year before the 1784 reprinting of the *Brief Narrative*, Erskine had made Zengerian arguments before Chief Justice Mansfield while unsuccessfully appealing the conviction of William Davies Shipley, dean of St.

Asaph, who had been prosecuted for urging parliamentary reform.[131] Although Erskine lost his legal case before the Court of King's Bench, he was subsequently vindicated by Parliament, which adopted many of his positions with the passage of Fox's Libel Act in 1792.[132] The 1784 edition of the *Brief Narrative* recognized the importance of Zenger's case in the struggle for a free press. While Zenger's case may not have been an important precedent for judges, as late as 1784 English politicians, publicists, lawyers, and jurors apparently thought it useful to the cause of freedom of expression.

On the American side of the Atlantic, Zenger's case affected the events surrounding the Revolution and influenced the writing of the Constitution. For example, the memory of the controversy in New York over the firing of Chief Justice Lewis Morris helped confirm in American minds, and doubtless in English minds as well, the importance of an independent judiciary made up of jurists appointed during good behavior. This contributed to the creation of an independent judiciary in the U.S. Constitution, as well as to the concept of the separation of powers.[133]

Most important, the Zenger controversy and trial served as an important precedent for those Americans demanding a bill of rights to guarantee freedom of the press, a trial by jury, a grand jury indictment before a trial, and the right to counsel. Leonard Levy has shown that American libel law did not change immediately after Zenger's case, and yet after the Zenger trial no colonial governor attempted to prosecute his critics for libel. Although the law on the books did not change, the political climate did. In this period, Americans did not develop a consistent free press ideology, but for the most part they understood and supported the notion that people should be able to criticize the government, *especially* the appointed royal governors. A full-blown free press ideology could only be worked out over time and with the experience gained from the Revolution, self-government, and the development of political parties. But the availability of Zenger's *Narrative* and the memory of Zenger's victory influenced the creation of the new republic and the securing of a free press.[134] Throughout the last six decades of the eighteenth century, lawyers and writers in America and Great Britain made Zengerian arguments in favor of freedom of the press and the right of the jury to decide guilt or innocence in a libel trial.[135]

In the years leading up to the Revolution, Zenger became something of an icon for many publishers. In 1766, New York City journalist John Holt, the "favorite printer" of the Sons of Liberty, renamed his paper after Zenger's, calling it the *New York Journal*.[136] When Alexander

McDougall was indicted for libel in 1770, Holt reprinted the Zenger narrative, reminding New York jurors of their right to determine both the law and the facts in a libel case. Holt's edition also contained an essay on the rights of juries and an abbreviated account of the trial of William Owen. The epigram at the front of this publication quoted Tiberius Caesar: "In a free State, such as ours is, all Men ought to enjoy, and express their Minds freely."[137]

During the debate over the ratification of the Constitution in 1787–1788, Americans again recalled Zenger's trial. Many Antifederalists opposed the Constitution because it lacked a bill of rights protecting fundamental liberties. In calling for libertarian amendments, "A Democratic Federalist" argued that "there is no knowing what corrupt and wicked judges may do in process of time, when they are not restrained by express law." After this discussion of his fears of corruption, the anonymous author reminded his readers that "the case of *John Peter Zenger* of New-York, ought still be present in our minds, to convince us how displeasing the liberty of the press is to men in high power."[138] Similarly, "Cincinnatus" asked what might happen if, in the future, "a patriotic printer, like Peter Zenger, should incur the resentment of our new rulers, by publishing to the world, transactions which they wish to conceal?" Cincinnatus complained that the new Constitution "provides no security for the freedom of the press" and that it did not guarantee "the security of trial by jury" for printers, even though "it was the jury only that saved Zenger."[139]

After the adoption of the Bill of Rights, the meaning of the First Amendment, with its protection of freedom of the press, remained unclear. In 1798, Congress adopted the infamous Sedition Act, which made it a crime to criticize the president. This law surely was in tension with the philosophy behind the Zenger case, that in a republic the people must be free to criticize their government. At the same time, however, the Sedition Act formally incorporated the principles that Andrew Hamilton had asserted in court. The new act allowed juries to determine both the facts and the law in a libel case and also allowed the defendant to argue the truth of the allegedly libelous statements. In the next two years, as the Adams administration prosecuted opposition printers and critics, many Americans revisited the Zenger narrative, reminding themselves that the essence of the Zenger case was not the role of the jury but the principle of free expression.

In 1799, at the height of the controversy over the Sedition Act, a Boston publisher again reprinted the *Brief Narrative*.[140] At that time, the law had only begun to accept Zengerian principles, but the people had been reading and learning about them for decades. Indeed, in the sixty-five years between Zenger's case and the expiration of the Sedition Act in 1801 there were some important sedition trials. Royal governors persecuted some colonial publishers, but more often, it seems, colonial legislatures ordered prosecutions of journalists who offended the lawmakers. During the Revolution, patriot prosecutors and juries persecuted Tory publishers for the content of their papers, although the number of these cases is quite small. Even under the Sedition Act, the Zengerian legacy of grand and petit jury resistance to seditious libel prosecutions remained vigorous. The Adams administration arranged for the arrest of twenty-five of its critics but could obtain only seventeen indictments and just ten convictions.

Despite the vigor and combativeness of the pre-Revolutionary and early national press, surprisingly few publishers and writers actually felt the direct force of the law. If this period left us a "legacy of suppression," as Leonard Levy has argued, it is a rather small legacy.[141] One reason for the paucity of sedition prosecutions was Zenger's case. Americans knew about it, for political leaders, lawyers, and concerned citizens in each generation had read reprints of the *Brief Narrative*. Even Levy, who deprecates the importance of the trial, admits that "with the possible exception of *Cato's Letters*," the *Brief Narrative* was "the most widely known source of libertarian thought in England and America during the eighteenth century."[142]

Zenger's victory made royal governors reluctant to persecute the colonial press. Grand juries might not indict, and petit juries might not convict in such cases. While the colonial legislatures continued to prosecute libels, Stanley N. Katz has pointed out that even in this, "progress had been made, for it is one thing to be prosecuted and judged by one's elected representatives and quite another to be assailed by the surrogates of the Crown."[143] Moreover, the colonial legislatures "perceived themselves as guardians of the people's rights." Indeed, in England the "parliamentary privilege" of punishing critics of Parliament "had developed historically out of an actual need to protect members from the displeasure of the monarch and government officials."[144] Thus, legislative prosecutions, while clearly repressive from a modern perspective, had grown out of the struggle against repression by the monarchy.

Libel suits continued to fetter the press and were inconsistent with modern notions of liberty. But the period between 1760 and 1801 was one of revolution and dramatic legal and political change. That a Tory printer facing the wrath of a patriot jury might be punished in the 1770s and 1780s is not surprising. We must never forget that it was a revolution they were fighting,[145] and it would be an unusual revolution that fully respected the civil liberties of the leaders of the old regime while the war was in progress. This is especially true because the Revolution also resembled a civil war, with neighbors fighting each other and no fixed battle or territorial lines, and thus the revolutionaries felt it necessary to suppress speech that might directly affect the war where it was being fought. Similarly, since the notion of a legitimate, nonseditious political opposition did not develop until after the Adams administration, it is not really surprising that a few Jeffersonians were prosecuted.

What is most important about the Zenger legacy is not that it brought an immediate and total change in the law of libel — it did not — but rather that in the Revolutionary and early national period, it was always there as a beacon for those who were gradually developing an ideology of freedom of expression. While the Revolution was being won in the "hearts and minds of the people," to use John Adams's apt phrase, the idea of a press free to criticize the government was constantly before the people in the form of the *Brief Narrative.*

IN THE COURT OF HISTORY

Zenger's attorneys argued for the right of a printer to publish the "truth" about public officials. Furthermore, they argued that a jury, not a judge, should decide whether a publication was in fact libelous. Congress accepted that standard in enacting the Sedition Act of 1798. That law showed that these protections were extremely flimsy. Political opinions are neither true nor false, although some political opinions may be based on "facts" that are objectively false. Nevertheless, juries, often stacked with Federalists, convicted some Jeffersonian printers and politicians for their opinions about President Adams.[146] Significantly, during the Sedition Act controversy, opponents of President Adams reissued the *Brief Narrative.*

The popular opposition to the Sedition Act of 1798 (as well as the failure of John Adams to win reelection in 1800) more or less ended seditious libel prosecutions, although Jefferson and his supporters briefly prosecuted Federalist publishers in New York, Pennsylvania, and New England.[147] However, during World War I, superpatriotic xenophobia, and the need of the Wilson administration to convince the nation that the War to End All Wars required American support, led to a new sedition act. Curiously, during World War I no one reissued the Zenger narrative to remind Americans of their heritage of freedom of expression. On the eve of American entrance into World War II, however, the *Brief*

Narrative reappeared in two editions. One, published by the Works Projects Administration, noted in its preface that "today, of all days, it is well to remember" the "inspirational words" of Andrew Hamilton that "liberty" is "the only bulwark against lawless power, which in all ages has sacrificed to its wild lust and boundless ambition the blood of the best men that ever lived."[148] These new editions of Zenger may have been a response to the suppression of free speech in Nazi Germany, fascist Italy, and the USSR. But with many Americans assuming that the United States would soon enter the war already raging in Europe and Asia, they may have been published as a caution to Americans not to repeat the suppression of free speech that took place in World War I. During the era of Senator Joseph McCarthy in the early 1950s, when freedom of expression was once again under severe attack, two more editions of the Zenger narrative appeared.[149]

In 1964, in the landmark case of *New York Times v. Sullivan*, the U.S. Supreme Court finally resolved the issue of seditious libel in favor of freedom of expression. In that case, the Court found that the Sedition Act of 1798 had been overruled by the "court of history."[150] In his concurring opinion, Justice Arthur Goldberg quoted Andrew Hamilton's arguments in the Zenger trial to support the proposition that those who fought the American Revolution understood the necessity of allowing the people to criticize the government.[151]

Today editors no longer need to prove the truth of their publications. Instead, politicians and other public officials who wish to sue the news media must prove that an editor or author "showed reckless disregard for the truth" or published something that was "knowingly false."[152] These high standards have led to a vigorous free press. As Chief Justice William Rehnquist said in *Hustler Magazine, Inc. v. Falwell*, "Despite their sometimes caustic nature, from the early cartoons portraying George Washington as an ass down to the present day, graphic depictions and satirical cartoons have played a prominent role in public and political debate. . . . From the viewpoint of history it is clear that our political discourse would have been considerably poorer without them."[153] Zenger's authors drew their cartoons with words rather than pictures, but the result was the same: Cosby was described as a monkey; his chief publicist, Francis Harison, was called a spaniel.

The use of the Zenger case has not been limited to the U.S. Supreme Court. In 2002, the Pennsylvania Supreme Court, in determining the meaning of freedom of expression under the state constitution, noted that "Philadelphia lawyer Andrew Hamilton's defense of John Peter Zenger played no less direct a role in both the federal and Pennsylvania protection of the freedom of the press and, hence, expression."[154] As modern courts understand, the heritage of the Zenger case is a proud and vital one for our political system. Despite the protection of freedom of the press, the idea of dangerous publications is still around. President Richard Nixon tried to suppress the Pentagon Papers, not because they threatened national security but rather because their publication threatened the reputation of the government. The CIA and other national security agencies have suppressed some publications through prior restraints.[155] In light of these developments, the *Brief Narrative* remains more than just a historical document. It retains its status, as it has for more than 250 years, as a key text in the struggle to create an open government, a vigorous press, and a free society.

NOTES

[1] *Jones v. U.S.*, 526 U.S. 227, 246 (1999); *McIntyre v. Ohio Election Commission*, 514 U.S. 334, 361 (1995).

[2] Stanley N. Katz, ed., *A Brief Narrative of the Case and Trial of John Peter Zenger: Printer of the* New York Weekly Journal, *by James Alexander*, 2nd ed. (Cambridge, Mass.: Harvard University Press, 1972), 37.

[3] Arthur M. Schlesinger Sr., *Prelude to Independence: The Newspaper War on Britain, 1764–1776* (New York: Alfred A. Knopf, 1958), 65.

[4] Morris quoted in Howard Adams, *Gouverneur Morris: An Independent Life* (New Haven, Conn.: Yale University Press, 2003), 11. Gouverneur Morris was Lewis Morris's grandson, and his prominence in the founding of the United States is one more example of how the Zenger case, and Zenger's supporters, helped pave the way for the Revolution.

[5] William Blackstone, *Commentaries on the Laws of England* (Oxford: Clarendon Press, 1765–1769), 4:150. Blackstone (1723–1780) was the first law professor in the Anglo-American world and held the Vinerian Professorship at Oxford. He is best known for this treatise, which was based on his Oxford lectures.

[6] Quoted in Schlesinger, *Prelude to Independence*, 115, 116.

[7] Bernard Bailyn, *The Ideological Origins of the American Revolution* (Cambridge, Mass.: Harvard University Press, 1967), 43. See also David L. Jacobson, ed., *The English Libertarian Heritage: From the Writings of John Trenchard and Thomas Gordon in* The Independent Whig *and* Cato's Letters (Indianapolis: Bobbs-Merrill, 1965).

[8] *John Peter Zenger: Defender of Freedom of the Press* (N.p.: Eastern National Park and Monument Association, n.d.), 5.

[9] Stephen Botein, *"Mr. Zenger's Malice and Falsehood": Six Issues of the* New-York Weekly Journal, *1733–34* (Worcester, Mass.: American Antiquarian Society, 1985), 8.

[10] *The arguments of the Council for the Defendant* (New York: John Peter Zenger, 1733); *The Proceedings of Rip Van Dam, Esq; in order for obtaining Equal Justice of His Excellency William Cosby, Esq.* (New York: John Peter Zenger, 1733). Zenger also printed three editions of Chief Justice Morris's opinion in the Van Dam case, *The Opinion and Argument of the Chief Justice of the Province of New-York, concerning the Jurisdiction of the supream Court of the said Province, to determine Causes in a Course of Equity*, 2nd ed., corrected and amended (New York: John Peter Zenger, 1733). The New York Public Library has two different versions of the "second edition" of this pamphlet. One, designated "2nd edition," is mispaginated and contains a list of "errata" on page 15. The other, designated "The Second Edition Corrected and Amended," is correctly paginated and contains no list of errata. This is in fact the third edition of the pamphlet.

¹¹ Zenger's name appears in a list of supporters of Morris that also included Rip Van Dam, James Alexander, Abraham De Peyster, Peter Bayard, and members of the Livingston, Beekman, Schuyler, and Gouverneur families—some of the wealthiest and most important families in the colony. Stanley N. Katz, *Newcastle's New York: Anglo-American Politics, 1732–1753* (Cambridge, Mass.: Harvard University Press, 1968), 95. The fact that Zenger was included in such a group suggests that he was seen as more than simply a tradesman setting type for a newspaper.

¹² *New York Weekly Journal*, January 7, 1734, quoted in Katz, *Brief Narrative*, 9.

¹³ Katz, *Brief Narrative*, 9.

¹⁴ Livingston Rutherfurd, *John Peter Zenger: His Press, His Trial and a Bibliography of Zenger Imprints* (New York: Dodd, Mead, 1904), 5.

¹⁵ See generally Katz, *Brief Narrative*, 15, and Leonard W. Levy, *The Emergence of a Free Press* (New York: Oxford University Press, 1985). Both works are based on earlier arguments the two authors set out in the 1960s: Katz's first edition of *A Brief Narrative* (Cambridge, Mass.: Harvard University Press, 1963) and Levy's *Legacy of Suppression: Freedom of Speech and the Press in Early America* (Cambridge, Mass.: Harvard University Press, 1960).

¹⁶ Donald L. Kemmerer, *Path to Freedom: The Struggle for Self-Government in Colonial New Jersey, 1703–1776* (Princeton, N.J.: Princeton University Press, 1940), 140.

¹⁷ For Cosby's background, see generally Katz, *Newcastle's New York*.

¹⁸ Dongan quoted in Hugh Hastings, ed., *Ecclesiastical Records of the State of New York* (Albany, N.Y.: James B. Lyon, State Printer, 1901), 2:879–80. See also Douglas Greenberg, *Crime in the Colony of New York* (Ithaca, N.Y.: Cornell University Press, 1978), 26.

¹⁹ The New York Council, or Governor's Council, functioned as both the upper house of the provincial legislature and the colonial equivalent of the king's Privy Council.

²⁰ Eugene R. Sheridan, *Lewis Morris, 1671–1746: A Study in Early American Politics* (Syracuse, N.Y.: Syracuse University Press, 1981), 148.

²¹ Ibid.; William Smith Jr., *The History of the Province of New-York by William Smith Jr.*, ed. Michael Kammen (Cambridge, Mass.: Harvard University Press, 1972), 2:5. Smith, the son of Zenger's lawyer William Smith, published his history in 1757.

²² Sheridan, *Lewis Morris*, 154–55.

²³ Ibid., 5–6; Katz, *Newcastle's New York*, 63.

²⁴ In the modern United States, for example, a suit to recover damages for personal injury—such as injuries suffered in a car accident—would be a common-law suit, in which the jury would determine who was at fault and what the monetary damages ought to be.

²⁵ Smith, *History of the Province of New-York*, 5.

²⁶ In England the chancellor was often a bishop or an archbishop whose job was to seek fairness and be the king's conscience. As such a chancery court might rule against the government in a case. But since the king could not be personally subject to a suit, there was never a direct conflict between the king's personal wealth and interests in such a suit. In the New York colony the governor represented the king and thus took on the role of the chancellor because there was no one else to appoint to that role. However, because Governor Cosby had initiated this civil suit on his own, he would have been in the odd position of being the judge in his own case, if the suit was heard in a chancery court.

²⁷ Jill Lepore, *New York Burning: Liberty, Slavery, and Conspiracy in Eighteenth-Century Manhattan* (New York: Alfred A. Knopf, 2005), 71; Katz, *Newcastle's New York*, 63–64.

²⁸ *Proceedings in the Case of Ship-Money, between the King and John Hampden, Esq.*, 3 Howell's State Trials 826 (1637). Hampden became a symbol of resistance to arbitrary royal rule. See Esther S. Cope, *Politics without Parliament, 1629–1640* (London: Allen & Unwin, 1987), 117–20. Significantly, Andrew Hamilton referred to Hampden's case in

urging the jury to protect liberty by acquitting Zenger. See p. 110 in this edition of *Brief Narrative*.

²⁹Stanley Katz, "The Politics of Law in Colonial America: Controversies over Chancery Courts and Equity Law in the Eighteenth Century," *Perspectives in American History* 5 (1971): 257–84.

³⁰Morris quoted in Sheridan, *Lewis Morris*, 149.

³¹Rutherfurd, *John Peter Zenger*, 10.

³²Ibid., 13.

³³*The Opinion and Argument of the Chief Justice of the Province of New-York, concerning the Jurisdiction of the supream Court.*

³⁴*Opinion and Argument of the Chief Justice; The arguments of the Council for the Defendant, In Support of Plea to the Jurisdiction Pleaded to a Bill filed in a Court of Equity, at the suit of the Attorney General, Complainant, Against Rip Van Dam, Defendant, in the Supream Court of New-York* (New York: John Peter Zenger, 1733).

³⁵*Opinion and Argument of the Chief Justice*, 7, 13 [emphasis in the original].

³⁶Sheridan, *Lewis Morris*, 149–51. See also *Opinion and Argument of the Chief Justice*. Morris's opinion was a careful work of legal scholarship, replete with references to *Coke's Institutes, The Case of the Earl of Darby*, 12 Coke 114; *Chutes Case*, 12 Coke 116; and numerous cases and statutes from England and New York. Jill Lepore notes that since 1691, "every successive governor and Assembly" had been "in a stalemate, with each insisting that it had the right to establish courts but neither willing to challenge the other." Lepore, *New York Burning*, 70.

³⁷Sheridan, *Lewis Morris*, 149. Morris (1671–1746) inherited vast wealth, including 6,200 acres in New Jersey and nearly 2,000 acres in New York, which were known as "Morrisania" and which today constitute much of the Bronx and Westchester County. His marriage in 1691 to Isabella Graham, the daughter of the Speaker of the New York Assembly, solidified his political prospects. He served in various elected and appointed positions in New Jersey and New York before becoming chief justice of the New York Supreme Court in 1715. Morris was one of the leading intellectuals in New York. He read Greek, Latin, Hebrew, and Arabic and built a private library of some three thousand volumes. In addition to his political writings and legal opinions, he wrote poetry, played the violin, and collected natural science specimens. Governor Cosby removed Morris as chief justice in 1733, which led to the Zenger case. In 1738, however, Morris became royal governor of New Jersey. His grandson Gouverneur Morris was one of the most active delegates to the Constitutional Convention, while another grandson, Lewis Morris III, was a signer of the Declaration of Independence.

³⁸Cosby to Newcastle, quoted in Sheridan, *Lewis Morris*, 151. For a discussion of Morris's declining political power, see Katz, *Newcastle's New York*, 73.

³⁹De Lancey (1703–1760) served as chief justice of the New York Supreme Court for the rest of his life. He also served as lieutenant governor of New York from 1753 until his death, as acting governor from 1753 to 1755, and as the de facto governor from 1757 until his death. His nephew and namesake, James De Lancey (1747–1804), was one of the most notorious Tories in New York during the Revolution; he escaped to Canada at the end of the war.

⁴⁰Katz, *Brief Narrative*, 1–2.

⁴¹Patricia U. Bonomi, *A Factious People: Politics and Society in Colonial New York* (New York: Columbia University Press, 1971), 114.

⁴²*New York Weekly Journal*, quoted in ibid. At this time, there was no secret ballot. Voters were asked, or "polled," with all other voters and candidates looking on.

⁴³Bonomi, *Factious People*, 114–15; *New York Weekly Journal*, quoted in ibid., 115. See also Vincent Buranelli, *The Trial of Peter Zenger* (New York: New York University Press, 1957), 23. The U.S. Constitution specifically allows for people to take office by "oath or affirmation," thus avoiding the problem of requiring people to "swear" an oath in violation of their religious beliefs.

⁴⁴Alexander (1691–1756) had emigrated from Scotland in 1715. As the surveyor general of the Jerseys and New York, he acquired valuable landholdings. His marriage in 1721 to Mary Spratt Provoost, a wealthy widow, brought him important commercial connections while providing cash for his land speculations. He would be disbarred during the Zenger crisis, but he returned to law practice after Governor Cosby's death in 1736. Alexander helped Benjamin Franklin found the American Philosophical Society in 1743 and was a founder of the New York Society Library in 1754, a vestryman of New York City's Trinity Church, and a founding trustee of King's College (now Columbia University). He was one of the wealthiest men in New York (worth £100,000 in 1745) and remained a staunch supporter of colonial rights. During the Revolution, his only son, William Alexander, carried on this tradition, serving as a major general in the American army.

⁴⁵The New York City Council should not be confused with the New York Council, or Governor's Council. The New York City Council (which included the Quarter Sessions) served as the legislature for the city of New York, just as a modern city council does.

⁴⁶Alexander to Robert Hunter, November 8, 1733, quoted in Katz, *Newcastle's New York*, 75.

⁴⁷Sheridan, *Lewis Morris*, 157–58; Smith, *History of the Province of New-York*, 8.

⁴⁸*New York Weekly Journal*, reprinted in Katz, *Brief Narrative*, 117–19.

⁴⁹See Buranelli, *Trial of Peter Zenger*, 28.

⁵⁰*New York Weekly Journal*, November 26, 1733.

⁵¹Cosby had appointed Harison to the position of recorder, who functioned as the chief attorney for the city. Harison was a particularly unscrupulous politician who William Smith and James Alexander believed tried to frame them in order to have them hanged. Eben Moglen, "Considering *Zenger*: Partisan Politics and the Legal Profession in Provincial New York," *Columbia Law Review* 94 (June 1994): 1496, 1507–10.

⁵²*New York Weekly Journal*, March 18, 1735, quoted in Katz, *Brief Narrative*, 9.

⁵³*New York Weekly Journal*, February 4, 1734.

⁵⁴Richard Coote, Earl of Bellomont (1636–1701), was a member of Parliament from 1688 to 1695 and a supporter of William of Orange, who made him an Irish peer in 1689. While governor of New York, Massachusetts, and New Hampshire (1697–1701), Coote commissioned Captain William Kidd to suppress piracy, but he later had to arrest Kidd, who was himself a pirate. Coote so neglected the colony's finances that when he died, "New York was absolutely insolvent." Coote also had a "mean temper, a tactless instinct to vilify his opponents, a tendency toward poor judgment of people, and a proclivity to alienate potential allies unnecessarily." Michael Kammen, *Colonial New York: A History* (New York: Scribner's, 1975), 141.

⁵⁵Edward Hyde, Viscount Cornbury (1661–1723), was governor of New York (1702–1708), where "he was despised by contemporaries as the most venal of all the colonial governors." In 1708, royal authorities recalled Cornbury to London, where they imprisoned him for his corruption and tyrannical behavior in the colony. Ibid., 156–58.

⁵⁶Lord Neil Campbell (c. 1630–1692) served as governor of East Jersey for about three months in 1686–1687 before abruptly resigning and returning to Scotland. His tenure as governor was a failure, though not marked by any particular scandal.

⁵⁷Philip Carteret (1639–1682) was the first governor of New Jersey, arriving in August 1665. Dutch settlers in the colony accepted his authority, but New Englanders who had settled there opposed his governorship. Many New Jersey colonists eventually defied his attempts to collect quitrents (fixed rents), leading to a short-lived rebellion. Carteret was later arrested by soldiers from New York in a dispute over his power to collect taxes. Throughout his administration, opponents claimed that he exceeded his legal authority. He gave up power in 1682.

⁵⁸Rutherfurd, *John Peter Zenger*, 32.

⁵⁹Quoted in Bonomi, *Factious People*, 113.

[60] *New York Weekly Journal*, January 21, 1734.

[61] *New York Weekly Journal*, January 14, 1734, cited in Elizabeth Christine Cook, *Literary Influences in Colonial Newspapers, 1704–1750* (New York: Columbia University Press, 1904), 126.

[62] *De Libellis Famosis*, 5 Coke's Rep. 125a, 77 Eng. Rep. 250 (1606).

[63] *Rex v. Tutchin*, 14 Howell's State Trials, 1095, 1128 (1704).

[64] Blackstone, *Commentaries on the Laws of England*, 4:150. This was not true for a private libel, where Blackstone noted that, "upon a civil action, the truth of the accusation may be pleaded in bar of the suit." Ibid.

[65] William Hawkins, *A Treatise on the Pleas of the Crown* (London: J. Walthoe, 1716), 1:194, sec. 6, quoted on p. 88.

[66] *Some Observations on the Charge given by the Honorable James De Lancey, Esq. Chief Justice of the Province of New-York, to the Grand Jury, the 15th Day of January, 1733* (New York: John Peter Zenger, 1734).

[67] The last three lines of each issue read: "NEW-YORK: Printed and Sold by *John Peter Zenger*. By whom Subscriptions for this Paper are taken at three Shillings *per* Quarter; and Advertisements at three Shillings the first Week, and one Shilling every Week after."

[68] From p. 54 in this edition.

[69] Katz, *Brief Narrative*, 18, 224.

[70] See p. 55 in this edition.

[71] From p. 60 in this edition.

[72] See pp. 56–59 in this edition.

[73] See pp. 59–60 in this edition.

[74] From p. 60 in this edition.

[75] Latin for "you should have the body." A writ "directed to any one having a person in his custody or under his restraint, commanded him to produce such person at a certain time and place, and to state the reasons why he is held in custody, or under restraint." John Bouvier, *A Law Dictionary Adapted to the Constitution and Laws of the United States of America* (Philadelphia: T. & J. W. Johnson, 1839), 1:454. Known as the "great writ," habeas corpus helps prevent arbitrary arrests and incarcerations by requiring that the persons arrested be brought before a judge to determine if there is a reason for holding the person in custody.

[76] See p. 61 in this edition.

[77] By this time, Morris was in England, lobbying unsuccessfully to have Cosby removed from office and to get back his position as chief justice. Considering his vast wealth, he also could have posted bail for Zenger.

[78] Alexander, with the help of Zenger's family, kept the paper going while Zenger awaited trial. Thus, people knew what was happening in the case. The pro-Cosby *New York Gazette* taunted the Morris faction for not bailing Zenger out. But the continued publication of Zenger's paper gave his supporters an opportunity to refute the pro-Cosby charges. An additional reason for not bailing Zenger out was the fear that Cosby would then arrest others in the opposition and perhaps tie up all their money with outrageous bail demands — bail that would later be forfeited if the government convicted those arrested. See Katz, *Brief Narrative*, 18–20, for a discussion of this.

[79] Sheridan, *Lewis Morris*, 163.

[80] From p. 61 in this edition.

[81] Informations are still used for certain prosecutions. For example, most traffic offenses are technically informations filed by the officer issuing the ticket. Only prosecutions for the most serious traffic offenses, usually those involving death or leaving the scene of an accident, require a grand jury indictment.

[82] *Assembly Journals*, 1:501, 600, quoted in *Documents Relative to the Colonial History of the State of New York*, ed. E. B. O'Callaghan, vol. 6 (Albany, N.Y.: Weed, Parsons, 1855), 17*n*.

[83] Ibid., 17–18.

84 Ibid., 18.

85 Levy, *Legacy of Suppression*, 129; Levy, *Emergence of a Free Press*, 39.

86 On Colden's role in the paper, see Katz, *Newcastle's New York*, 75.

87 Leonard W. Levy, *Origins of the Fifth Amendment: The Right against Self-Incrimination* (New York: Oxford University Press, 1968), 266–332, discusses the case of Lilburne. See also Pauline Gregg, *Free-Born John: A Biography of John Lilburne* (London: Harrap, 1961), and Michael Kent Curtis, *Free Speech, "The People's Darling Privilege": Struggles for Freedom of Expression in American History* (Durham, N.C.: Duke University Press, 2000). The Star Chamber imprisoned Lilburne for his opposition to the regime of King Charles I and for his religious beliefs.

88 Buranelli, *Trial of Peter Zenger*, 38–39, asserts that Zenger's wife, Anna Catharina Zenger, published the paper. There is no contemporary evidence to support this assertion, nor is there any indication that she was trained as a printer. Zenger's sons had worked with their father before his arrest, and his eldest son would eventually take over the printing business. However, in the two years after Zenger died (in 1746), Catharine (as she spelled her name) became the proprietor of the Zenger press and produced at least one book with the imprint "Printed and Sold by the Widow Catharine Zenger." In 1735, she may very well have functioned as the business manager for her husband. In 1748, she turned the business over to her stepson, John Zenger Jr., who ran the press until his death in 1751. Charles R. Hildeburn, *Sketches of Printers and Printing in Colonial New York* (New York: Dodd, Mead, 1895), 29–32.

89 Isaiah Thomas, *The History of Printing in America* (Worcester, Mass.: The Press of Isaiah Thomas, Jun., Isaac Sturtevant, printer, 1810; repr., Barre, Mass.: Imprint Society, 1970).

90 Moglen, "Considering *Zenger*," makes a similar point, p. 1513.

91 "Order of the King in Council declaring the Reasons for removing Chief Justice Morris insufficient," November 26, 1735, in *Documents Relative to the Colonial History of the State of New York*, 6:36–37.

92 From p. 63 in this edition. "During good behavior" implies that a judge will serve for life, or until retirement, unless the judge is removed by impeachment or through some other official proceeding for misbehavior. This is the standard for federal judges in the United States today. The opposite of "during good behavior" is "during pleasure" or "at pleasure," which means a judge or other official serves at the whim of the chief executive. This is the standard for members of the president's cabinet, who may be removed whenever the president chooses.

93 Lewis Morris to the Lords of Trade, August 27, 1733, in *Documents Relative to the Colonial History of the State of New York*, 5:954.

94 From p. 63 in this edition.

95 Ibid. They also argued that for similar reasons, the commission of Frederick Philipse was invalid.

96 Moglen, "Considering *Zenger*," 1515–16, suggests that had the attack on the commissions been successful, it might have shut down the court altogether, because contrary to English law, neither Parliament nor the New York legislature had passed a statute re-creating the court after the death of King George I and the ascension of George II. Chief Justice De Lancey certainly saw it this way. After a brief discussion of his commission, De Lancey declared, "*You have brought it to that Point, That either, We must go from the Bench, or you from the Barr.*" From p. 65 in this edition.

97 From pp. 65, 66, and 67 in this edition.

98 Chambers might also have been hedging his bets here. Sooner or later (and it turned out to be relatively sooner, since Cosby died in March 1736), Cosby would leave office, and at that point Chambers might need the patronage or support of Morris and Alexander, or at least not want their enmity. After all, the next governor might be their ally. Furthermore, the Morrisites had just swept the colonial elections, and being on relatively good terms with them had some value.

⁹⁹From p. 69 in this edition.
¹⁰⁰See p. 70 in this edition. Chambers took his role as defense attorney seriously, trying to win the case despite his ties to the governor. This illustrates the complicated question of how politically active lawyers behave when they are involved in political trials. In this case, Chambers upheld the integrity of his profession (and himself) at the expense of the political faction with which he was allied. Although Chief Justice De Lancey was intent on seeing Zenger convicted, the crude misbehavior of the sheriff also offended De Lancey's view of the integrity of the legal system. De Lancey could not have ruled otherwise without fundamentally rejecting accepted legal precedents and practice. Furthermore, De Lancey doubtless believed that since he had removed Zenger's attorneys, there was little chance that the prosecution would fail. Thus, he could afford to make it appear to be a fair trial.
¹⁰¹Significantly, half of the jurors were of Dutch ancestry and were probably likely to be particularly supportive of Zenger and his Dutch patron, Rip Van Dam. However, Katz notes that the jurors were "properly struck from the Freeholders' Book in the presence of counsel." Katz, *Brief Narrative*, 21. If this was so, the jurors, while sympathetic to Zenger, were also chosen from a cross section of New York property holders. Historians have identified six of the jurors, including the foreman, Thomas Hunt, as men with ties to the Morris faction. Ibid., 21–22.
¹⁰²Katz, *Brief Narrative*, 22–23, 29, 35, 37; Levy, *Legacy of Suppression*, 50–53, 130–33.
¹⁰³From pp. 75 and 82 in this edition.
¹⁰⁴From p. 82 in this edition.
¹⁰⁵Hamilton was probably lucky that the court did not accept his offer, since some of Zenger's attacks on the governor were exaggerated or untrue.
¹⁰⁶From p. 87 in this edition.
¹⁰⁷From p. 88 in this edition. The Star Chamber had been the court of the monarch's Privy Council. This court had operated without a jury, formal indictments, or any other traditional common-law rule. King James I (r. 1603–1625) and King Charles I (r. 1625–1649) had used it to suppress political and religious (especially Puritan) dissidents. In 1641, on the eve of the English Civil War (1642–1651), the Long Parliament abolished this notoriously arbitrary court. However, Star Chamber precedents, especially the case of *Libellis Famosis*, remained good law in England until after Zenger's case was decided.
¹⁰⁸From p. 88 in this edition. Some of the accusations in Zenger's paper were not in fact true, but the attorney general could not afford to pursue this question because enough of Zenger's paper was true to thoroughly embarrass the Cosby administration.
¹⁰⁹From p. 107 in this edition [italics and brackets in the original], quoting Isaiah 9:16.
¹¹⁰From p. 107 in this edition, quoting Isaiah 56:10–11.
¹¹¹From p. 111 in this edition. It seems likely that the presence of "the People" in the courtroom had ensured that De Lancey would not disbar Hamilton or even prevent him from making his arguments directly to the jury.
¹¹²From p. 112 in this edition.
¹¹³From pp. 114–116 in this edition. See also Thomas, *History of Printing in America*, 487–90. On the decline of the Morris faction, see Katz, *Newcastle's New York*; Bonomi, *Factious People*, 140–78; Moglen, "Considering *Zenger*," 1496; and Rutherfurd, *John Peter Zenger*, 128–31.
¹¹⁴Levy, *Emergence of a Free Press*, 44.
¹¹⁵Levy, *Legacy of Suppression*, 133.
¹¹⁶From p. 80 in this edition.
¹¹⁷From pp. 80–81 in this edition.
¹¹⁸Hamilton argued:"I believe it would be looked upon as a strange Attempt, for one Man here, to bring an Action against another, whose Cattle and Horses feed upon his

Grounds not inclosed, or indeed for eating and treading down his Corn, if that were not inclosed. Numberless are the Instances of this Kind that might be given, to shew, that what is good Law at one Time and in one Place, is not so at another Time and in another Place; so that I think, the Law seems to expect, that in these Parts of the World Men should take Care, by a good Fence, to preserve their Property, from the Injury of unruly Beasts. And perhaps there may be a good Reason why Men should take the same Care, to make an honest and upright Conduct [as] a Fence and Security against the Injury of unruly Tongues." From pp. 81–82 in this edition.

[119] Anglo-Americanus [Jonathan Blenman], *Remarks on Zenger's Tryal, Taken out of the Barbados Gazette's: For the Benefit of the Students in Law, and Others in North America* (New York: William Bradford, 1737), reprinted in Katz, *Brief Narrative*, 152–80.

[120] Thomas, *History of Printing in America*, 432–36. Lawrence H. Leder, in *Liberty and Authority: Early American Political Ideology, 1689–1763* (Chicago: Quadrangle Press, 1968), 28–29, argues that Alexander "probably chose the Philadelphia newspaper because Hamilton, who had been the defense attorney, was being strenuously assaulted by his Pennsylvania enemies because of his role in the trial." Thus, Alexander's letters are not only a response to Anglo-Americanus but also a defense of Hamilton.

[121] Katz, *Brief Narrative*, 181.

[122] Ibid.

[123] *Remarks on the Trial of John-Peter Zenger, Printer of the* New York Weekly Journal, *Who was Lately Try'd and Acquitted for Printing and Publishing Two Libels Against the Government of that Province* (London: J. Roberts, 1738).

[124] Cook, *Literary Influences in Colonial Newspapers*, 139–40.

[125] Botein, *"Mr. Zenger's Malice and Falsehood,"* 5. The best source for the history of the reprinting of the Zenger narrative is Rutherfurd, *John Peter Zenger*, 249–55.

[126] Levy, *Emergence of a Free Press*, 156.

[127] Levy, *Legacy of Suppression*, 160, passim.

[128] Levy, *Emergence of a Free Press*, 156–57.

[129] Quoted in Rutherfurd, *John Peter Zenger*, 253.

[130] Thomas Erskine, quoted in Frederic S. Siebert, *Freedom of the Press in England, 1476–1776: The Rise and Decline of Government Control* (Urbana: University of Illinois Press, 1952), 392.

[131] *The Case of Rev. William Davies Shipley, Dean of St. Asaph, for a Seditious Libel*, 21 Howell's State Trials 847 (1783).

[132] Siebert, *Freedom of the Press in England*, 7, 288–92.

[133] See Moglen, "Considering *Zenger*," 1511, who makes a similar point.

[134] Levy argues that there were no theoretical discussions of the liberty of the press in the three decades after the Zenger case, and few after the outbreak of the Revolution, until the Sedition Act was passed in 1798. Levy, *Legacy of Suppression*, 140. But even Levy concedes the importance of the republication of the Zenger narrative.

[135] Levy, *Emergence of a Free Press*, 144–219.

[136] Stephen Botein, "Printers and the American Revolution," in *The Press and the American Revolution*, ed. Bernard Bailyn and John B. Hench (Worcester, Mass.: American Antiquarian Society, 1980), 28.

[137] Siebert, *Freedom of the Press in England*, 383; Rutherfurd, *John Peter Zenger*, 253.

[138] "A Democratic Federalist," *Pennsylvania Herald*, October 17, 1787, reprinted in *The Documentary History of the Ratification of the Constitution*, ed. John P. Kaminski and Gaspare J. Saladino (Madison: State Historical Society of Wisconsin, 1981), 13:388.

[139] "Cincinnatus I: To James Wilson, Esquire," *New York Journal*, November 1, 1787, reprinted in *Documentary History of Ratification*, 13:532–33.

[140] Rutherfurd, *John Peter Zenger*, 253.

[141] Levy, *Legacy of Suppression*, 19–248, and *Emergence of a Free Press*, 1–219, discusses the major libel prosecutions up to the Sedition Act. In all this period, there were fewer than twenty major prosecutions; many were of Tories. Levy acknowledges that

48INTRODUCTION

"a long war for independence hardly provides a propitious time for respecting, let alone nurturing, freedom of political expression or any civil liberties." *Emergence of a Free Press*, 173. He then goes on to detail suppression during the Revolution. He argues that there was no philosophy of freedom of the press until after the Sedition Act. This may be true, to the extent that no one laid out the arguments in detail. But the small number of prosecutions make it clear that there was a great deal of tolerance. Even the punishments were mild, compared to those in other revolutions. Indeed, given the massive number of prosecutions in the twentieth century, particularly during World War I, the colonial and Revolutionary period may offer us what is truly a legacy of toleration and freedom.

142 Levy, *Legacy of Suppression*, 133.

143 Katz, *Brief Narrative*, 31.

144 Jeffrey A. Smith, *Printers and Press Freedom: The Ideology of Early American Journalism* (New York: Oxford University Press, 1988), 8.

145 With apologies to Chief Justice John Marshall, who wrote in *McCulloch v. Maryland*, (17 U.S.) 316 (1819), "We must never forget that it is a Constitution we are expounding."

146 Consider, for example, Congressman Matthew Lyon, who was the first person convicted under the 1798 law and who complained that all the jurors at his trial came from districts that had voted against him. He believed that the U.S. marshal, a John Adams appointee, had personally selected the jurors. *Lyon's Case*, 15 F. Cas. 1183 (C.C.D. Vt. 1798).

147 There were still prosecutions at the state level. See Levy, *Emergence of a Free Press*, 338–49. In the most famous state prosecution, *People v. Croswell*, 3 Johns (N.Y.) 336 (1804), Alexander Hamilton cited Zenger's case for the proposition that in New York, truth was a legitimate defense to a libel prosecution. Hamilton argued that De Lancey's assertions that the jury could not find a general verdict on the basis of truth had been "reprobated at the time." Hamilton turned the whole notion of precedent inside out, asserting that a "single precedent" never forms the law," and thus the rulings of "a colonial judge, of a remove colony" could not "settle" the law. Julius Goebel, ed., *The Law Practice of Alexander Hamilton* (New York: Columbia University Press, 1964), 1:829. The Jefferson administration also prosecuted some Federalist editors using the common law of libel, even though in the 1790s Jefferson had argued there was no federal common law of crimes. In *United States v. Hudson and Goodwin*, 11 U.S. (7 Cr.) 32 (1812), the U.S. Supreme Court ruled that the federal government could not prosecute anyone without a statute, and thus the government dropped indictments against Barzillai Hudson and George Goodwin, who had attacked the Jefferson administration in the *Connecticut Currant*, a Federalist newspaper. Leonard W. Levy, *Jefferson and Civil Liberties: The Darker Side* (Cambridge, Mass.: Harvard University Press, 1963).

148 *The Trial of John Peter Zenger (1734) [sic] and the Freedom of the Press*, Works Projects Administration, A. Yedidia, Supervisor, California State Library, Sutro Branch, occasional papers, English series, no. 7 (San Francisco: California State Library, 1940), iv. Oddly, the WPA used as its source a 1765 London edition published by J. Almon. This edition grandly asserts in its preface that "Zenger was acquitted and the doctrine of the freedom of the press firmly established in the United States." Ibid. There was also a 1941 reprint of the Rutherfurd edition. Livingston Rutherfurd, *John Peter Zenger: His Press, His Trial and a Bibliography of Zenger Imprints* (New York: Peter Smith, 1941).

149 Frank Luther Mott, ed., *Oldtime Comments on Journalism*, vol. 2, *Zenger's Own Story: A Brief Narrative of the Case and Tryal of John Peter Zenger, Printer of the New-York Journal: A Literal Reprint of the Original Pamphlet Printed by Zenger in New York in 1736* (Columbia, Mo.: Press of the Crippled Turtle, 1954). Despite his title, Mott in fact added an introduction, headnotes, subtitles, and a number of notes to the text. Anticipating modern historical analysis, Mott noted that Zenger's case did not change the law, but rather that Hamilton's arguments "embodied legal doctrine far ahead of its time." Ibid.,

41. The second McCarthy-era edition was Buranelli, *Trial of Peter Zenger*, published in 1957. In his preface, Buranelli asserted that "freedom of the press is essential to our civilization" (iii).

[150] *New York Times v. Sullivan*, 376 U.S. 254, at 276 (1964).

[151] Ibid., 301.

[152] This is the standard set out in *New York Times v. Sullivan*.

[153] *Hustler Magazine, Inc. v. Falwell*, 485 U.S. 46 (1988).

[154] *Pap's A.M. T/DB/A Kandyland v. City of Erie*, 571 Pa. 375; 812 A.2d 591 (2002), at 398 (605).

[155] See Judith Schenck Koffler and Bennett L. Gershman, "National Security and Civil Liberties: The New Seditious Libel," *Cornell Law Review* 69 (1984): 816. See also *Snepp v. United States*, 444 U.S. 507 (1980), and *Haig v. Agee*, 453 U.S. 280 (1981). Prior restraint is the legal term for a government action that prevents an author from publishing his work. Thus the "restraint" on the publication is "prior" to its actual printing. Seditious libel prosecutions, by contrast, would be post-publication restraints, with the arrest of the author or publisher taking place *after* the allegedly libelous material is published. Before 1694 England required that all publications be licensed before they were printed. This allowed the government to prevent publication when it so desired (prior restraint).

A Brief Narrative of the Case and Tryal of John Peter Zenger, Printer of the *New-York Weekly Journal*

Zenger the Printer and an Angry Governor

The Narrative *opens with Zenger briefly stating the history of his publication of the* New York Weekly Journal *before recapitulating, in much more detail, Governor William Cosby's attempts through the New York Supreme Court and the Governor's Council to prosecute Zenger and suppress his newspaper. Here Zenger reprints a portion of Chief Justice James De Lancey's charge urging a grand jury to indict him for seditious libel, as well as several messages and resolutions from the council demanding action against him and his paper. (The recently appointed De Lancey had replaced one of Zenger's patrons, Lewis Morris.) What are the arguments against Zenger as stated in the various documents quoted here, and how persuasive are they? Would they have been less or more persuasive had James Alexander (the actual author of the* Narrative*) also included excerpts from the allegedly libelous newspaper articles?*

As There was but one Printer in the Province of *New-York*, that printed a publick News Paper, I was in Hopes, if I undertook to publish another, I might make it worth my while; and I soon found my Hopes were not groundless: My first Paper was printed, *Nov. 5th, 1733*, and I continued printing and publishing of them, I thought to the Satisfaction of every Body, till the *January* following: when the Chief Justice was pleased to animadvert[1] upon the Doctrine of Libels, in a long Charge given in that Term to the Grand Jury, and afterwards on the third *Tuesday* of *October, 1734*, was again pleased to charge the Grand Jury in the following Words.

Gentlemen; I shall conclude with reading a Paragraph or two out of the same Book, concerning Libels; they are arrived to that Height, that they call loudly for your Animadversion; it is high Time to put a Stop to them; for at the rate Things are now carried on, when all Order and Government is endeavoured to be trampled on; Reflections are cast upon Persons of all Degrees, must not these Things end in Sedition, if not timely prevented? Lenity, you have seen will not avail, it becomes you then to enquire after the Offenders, that we may in a due Course of Law be enabled to punish them. If you, *Gentlemen*, do not interpose, consider whether the ill Consequences that may arise from any Disturbances of the publick Peace, may not in part, lye at your Door?

Hawkins, in his Chapter of Libels,[2] considers three Points, *1st. What shall be said to be a Libel. 2dly. Who are lyable to be punished for it. 3dly. In what Manner they are to be punished.* Under the *1st. he says, §.7. Nor can there be any Doubt, but that a Writing which defames a private Person only, is as much a Libel as that which defames Persons entrusted in a publick Capacity, in as much as it manifestly tends to create ill Blood, and to cause a Disturbance of the publick Peace; however it is certain, that it is a very high Aggravation of a Libel, that it tends to scandalize the Government, by reflecting on those who are entrusted with the Administration of publick Affairs, which does not only endanger the publick Peace, as all other Libels do, by stirring up the Parties, immediately concerned in it, to Acts of Revenge, but also has a direct Tendency to breed in the People a Dislike of their Governours, and incline them to Faction and Sedition.* As to the *2d.* Point he says. §10 *It is certain, not only he who composes or procures another to compose it but also that he who publishes, or*

---

[1] *animadvert:* In this context, *animadvert* has an obsolete meaning of "to take notice of." However, the term also means "to comment unfavorably or critically" on something. Here the author is saying that Chief Justice De Lancey asked the grand jury to take notice of the law of libel. The author is implying that De Lancey was denouncing Zenger's act of libel and wanted the grand jury to charge him under "the Doctrine of Libels."

[2] The reference is to William Hawkins, *A Treatise of the Pleas of the Crown* (London: J. Wolthoe, 1716), 1:193–96.

procures another to publish it, are in Danger of being punished for it; and it is said not to be material whether he who disperses a Libel, knew any Thing of the Contents or Effects of it or not; for nothing could be more easy than to publish the most virulent Papers with the greatest Security, if the concealing the Purport of them from an illiterate Publisher,[3] would make him safe in the dispersing [of] them: Also, it has been said, that if he who hath either read a Libel himself, or hath heard it read by another, do afterwards maliciously read or report any Part of it in the Presence of others, or lend or shew it to another, he is guilty of an unlawful Publication of it. Also it hath been holden, that the Copying of a Libel shall be a conclusive Evidence of the Publication of it, unless the Party can prove, that he delivered it to a Magistrate to examine it, in which Case the Act subsequent is said to explain the Intention precedent. But it seems to be the better Opinion, that he who first writes a Libel, dictated by another, is thereby guilty of Making of it, and consequently punishable for the bare Writing; for it was no Libel till it was reduced to Writing.

These, *Gentlemen*, are some of the Offences which are to make Part of your Enquiries; and if any other should arise in the Course of your Proceedings, in which you are at a Loss, or conceive any Doubts, upon your Application here, We will assist and direct you.

The Grand Jury not indicting me as was expected, the Gentlemen of the Council proceeded to take my Journals into Consideration, and sent the following Message to the general Assembly.

Die Jovis, 3 ho. P.M. *17th of* October, 1734.[4]

A Message from the Council by *Philip Cortlandt*, in these Words, *to wit*,

That Board having had several of *Zenger's New-York weekly Journals*, laid before them, and other scurrilous Papers, tending to alienate the Affections of the People of this Province from His Majesty's Government, to raise Seditions and Tumults among the People of this Province, and to fill their Minds with a Contempt of His Majesty's Government: And considering the pernicious Consequences that may attend such growing Evils, if not speedily and effectually put a Stop to. And conceiving that the most likely Method to put a Stop to such bold and seditious Practices, to maintain the Dignity

---

[3]The idea of an "illiterate publisher" seems odd to modern readers, but in the early years of printing, some printers were simply typesetters who did not know how to read or could not read well. Some printers defended libel prosecutions by arguing that they had neither written nor read what they had published.
[4]Thursday, at 3:00 p.m.

of his Majesty's Government, and to preserve the Peace thereof, would be by a Conferrence between a Committee of this Board, and a Committee of the Assembly; it is therefore ordered, That the Gentlemen of this Board, NOW ASSEMBLED, of any seven of them, be a Committee, to join a Committee of the House of Representatives, in order to confer together, and to examine and enquire into the said Papers, and the Authors and Writers thereof.

Which Message being read.

Ordered, That the Members of this House, or any fourteen of them, do meet a Committee of the Council, at the Time and Place therein mentioned.

Die Veneris, 9 ho. 18 October, 1734.[5]

Mr. *Garretson* from the Committee of this House reported, That they last Night met the Committee of the Council, on the subject Matter of their Message of yesterday to this House; and that after several Preliminaries between the said Committees, the Gentlemen of the Council reduced to Writing, what they requested of this House, and delivered the same to the Chairman, who delivered it in at the Table, and being read, is in the Words following.

At a Committee of the Council held the *17th of October, 1734.*

PRESENT.

Mr. *Clarke.*	Mr. *Livingston.*	Mr. *Courtland.*
Mr. *Harison.*	Mr. *Kennedy.*	Mr. *Lane.*
Dr. *Colden.*	Mr. Chief Justice.	Mr. *Horsmanden.*

Gentlemen;

The Matters we request your Concurrence in, are, That *Zenger's* Papers, No. 7, 47, 48, 49,[6] which were read, and which we now deliver, be burnt by the Hands of the common Hangman, as containing in them many Things derogatory of the Dignity of His Majesty's Government, reflecting upon the Legislature, upon the most considerable Persons, in the most Distinguished Stations in the Province, and tending to raise Seditions and Tumults among the People thereof.

That you concur with us in the Addressing the Governour, to issue His Proclamation, with a Promise of Reward for the Discovery of the Authors or Writers of these Seditious Libels.

---

[5] Friday, at 9:00 a.m.
[6] See Document 2 on page 124.

That you concur with us in an Order for Prosecuting the Printer thereof.

That you concur with us in an Order to the Magistrates, to exert themselves in the Execution of their Offices, in order to preserve the publick Peace of the Province.

By Order of the Committee.

Fred. Morris, Cl. Con.[7]

Mr. *Garretson* delivered likewise to the House the several Papers referred to in the said Request.

Ordered, That the said Papers be lodg'd with the Clerk of this House, and that the Consideration thereof, and the said Request, be referred till *Tuesday* next.

Die Martis, 9 ho. A.M. *22 October, 1734.*[8]

The House according to Order proceeded to take into Consideration the Request of a Committee of Council, delivered to a Committee of this House, on the *16th* instant, as likewise of the several Papers therein referred to. And after several Debates upon the subject Matters, it was ORDERED THAT THE SAID PAPERS AND REQUEST LYE ON THE TABLE.

The Council finding the General Assembly would not do any Thing about it, they sent the following Message to the House.

Die Sabbati, 9 ho. A.M. *2 November, 1734*[9]

A Message from the Council by Mr. *Livingston,* desiring this House to return by him to that Board, the several seditious journals of *Zenger's* No. 7, 47, 48, 49, which were delivered by a Committee of that Board to a Committee of this House, the *17th* of *October* last, together with the Proposals of the Committee of that Board, delivered therewith to a Committee of this House; and then withdrew.

On *Tuesday* the *5th* of *November, 1734,* the *Quarter Sessions* for the City of *New-York* began, when the Sheriff delivered to the Court AN ORDER, which was read in these Words.[10]

At a Council held at Fort *George,* in *New-York,* the *2d* of *November, 1734.*

---

[7]Clerk of the Council.
[8]Tuesday, at 9:00 a.m.
[9]Saturday, at 9:00 a.m.
[10]The Quarter Sessions was the upper chamber of the New York City Council.

PRESENT.

His Excellency *Wiliam Cosby,* Capt. General and Governour in Chief, &c.

Mr. *Clark.*	Mr. *Livingston.*	Mr. *Cortland.*
Mr. *Harison.*	Mr. *Kennedy.*	Mr. *Lane.*
Dr. *Colden.*[11]	Mr. Chief Justice	Mr. *Horsmanden.*

Whereas by an Order of this Board, of this Day, some of John Peter Zenger's *Journals, entitled,* The New-York weekly Journal, containing the freshest Advices, foreign and domestick, No. 7, 47, 48, 49, *were ordered to be burnt by the Hands of the common Hangman, or Whipper, near the Pillory in this City, on* Wednesday *the* 6th *Instant, between the Hours of Eleven and Twelve in the Forenoon, as containing in them many Things tending to Sedition and Faction, to bring His Majesty's Government into Contempt, and to disturb the Peace thereof, and containing in them likewise, not only Reflections upon His Excellency the Governour in particular, the Legislature in general, but also upon the most considerable Persons in the most distinguished Stations in this Province. It is therefore ordered, That the Mayor, and Magistrates of this City, do attend at the Burning of the several Papers or Journals aforesaid, Numbered as above mentioned.*

Fred. Morris, D. Cl. Con.

To *Robert Lurting,* Esq; Mayor of the City of *New-York,* and the Rest of the Magistrates for the said City and County.

Upon reading of which ORDER, the Court forbad the Entring thereof in their Books at that Time, and many of them declared that if it should be entred, they would have their Protest entered against it.

On *Wednesday* the *6th* of *November,* the Sherriff of *New-York* moved the Court of *Quarter Sessions,* to comply with the said Order, upon which one of the Aldermen offered a protest, which was read by the Clerk, and approved of by all the Aldermen, either expressly or by not objecting to it, and is as followeth.

Whereas an ORDER has been served on this Court, in these Words.

[The Order as above incerted.]

And whereas this Court conceives, they are only to be commanded by the King's Mandatory Writs, authorized by Law, to

[11] N.B. Doctor Colden *was that day, at* Esopus [present-day Kingston, N.Y.], 90 *Miles from* New-York, *tho' mentioned as present in Council.* [Zenger]

which they conceive they have the Right of shewing Cause why they don't obey them, if they believe them improper to be obey'd, or by ORDERS, which have some known Laws to authorize them; and whereas this Court conceives THIS ORDER to be no Mandatory Writt warranted by Law, nor knows of no Law that authorizes the making the Order aforesaid; so they think themselves under no Obligation to obey it: Which Obedience, they think, would be in them, an opening [of] a Door for arbitrary Commands, which, when once opened, they know not what Dangerous Consequences may attend it. Wherefore this Court conceives it self bound in Duty (for the Preservation of the Rights of this Corporation, and as much as they can, the Liberty of the Press and the People of the Province, since an Assembly of the Province, and several Grand Juries, have refused to meddle with the Papers, when applied to by the Council) *to protest against the* ORDER *aforesaid, and to forbid all the Members of this Corporation, to pay any Obedience to it,* until it be shewn to this Court, that the same is Authorized by some known Law, which they neither know nor believe that it is.

Upon reading of which, it was required of the Honourable *Francis Harison,* Recorder of this Corporation,[12] and one of the Members of the Council, (present at making said Order) to shew by what Law or Authority that said ORDER was made; upon which he spoke in Support of it, and cited the Case of Doctor *Sacheverel's* Sermon,[13] which was by the House of Lords ordered to be burnt by the Hands of the Hangman, and that the Mayor and Aldermen of *London* should attend the doing of it, to which one of the Aldermen answered to this Purpose; that he conceived the Case was no ways parallel, because Doctor *Sacheverel,* and his Sermon, were impeached by the House of Commons of *England,* which is the Grand Jury of the Nation, and Representative of the whole People of *England*: That this their Impeachment they prosecuted before the House of Lords, the greatest Court of Justice of *Britain,* and which

[12]The recorder functioned as the chief attorney for the city. Harison was a particularly unscrupulous politician who William Smith and James Alexander believed tried to frame them in order to have them hanged. Zenger's paper vigorously attacked Harison, portraying him as a "spaniel," a dog loyal to the governor. Eben Moglen, "Considering Zenger: Partisan Politics and the Legal Profession in Provincial New York," *Columbia Law Review* 94 (June 1994): 1496, 1507–10.

[13]On February 27, 1710, the House of Lords convicted Reverend Henry Sacheverell for sermons that supported the divine right of kings and questioned parliamentary authority. The House of Commons had previously "impeached" Sacheverell for the sermons he had given in 1709. An "impeachment" in this case was the equivalent of an indictment, but one brought by the House of Commons, rather than by a grand jury. The House of Lords, after trying Sacheverell, ordered that his sermon be burned. See *The Trial of Henry Sacheverell,* 15 Howell's State Trials 1 (1710).

beyond Memory of Man, has had Cognizance of Things of that Nature, that there *Sacheverel* had a fair Hearing in Defence of himself and of his Sermon. And after that fair Hearing, he and his Sermon were justly, fairly and legally condemned; that he had read the Case of Dr. *Sacheverel,* & thought he could charge his Memory, that the Judgment of the House of Lords in that Case was, That the Mayor and Sheriffs of *London* and *Middlesex*, only should attend the Burning of the Sermon, and not the Aldermen; and farther he remembered, that the Order upon the Judgment, was only directed to the Sheriffs of *London*, and not even to the Mayor, who did not attend the doing it; and farther said, that would Mr. Recorder shew, that the Governour and Council had such Authority as the House of Lords, and that the Papers ordered to be burnt were in like manner legally prosecuted and condemned, there the Case of Doctor *Sacheverel* might be to the Purpose; but without shewing that, it rather proved that a Censure ought not to be pronounced, till a fair Tryal by a Competent and legal Authority were first had. Mr. Recorder was desired to produce the Books from whence he cited his Authorities, that the Court might judge of them themselves, and was told, that if he could produce sufficient Authorities to warrant *this ORDER*, they would readily obey it, but otherwise not. Upon which he said, he did not carry his Books about with him. To which it was answered, he might send for them, or order a Constable to fetch them. Upon which he arose, and at the lower End of the Table he mentioned, That Bishop *Burnet's* Pastoral Letter, was ordered by the House of Lords, to be burnt by the High Bailiff of *Westminster*;[14] upon which he abruptly went away, without waiting

---

[14]The reference here is to a letter written by the Scottish-born Gilbert Burnet, Bishop of Salisbury (1643–1715), who, in addition to his work as a clergyman, was the author of *Bishop Burnet's History of His Own Time: From the Restoration of King Charles the Second to the Treaty of Peace at Utrecht, in the Reign of Queen Anne,* 2 vols. (London: T. Ward, 1724–1734), and other historical works. Burnet was in exile during the reign of James II but returned to England with William and Mary in 1688 and preached their coronation sermon. In 1689, he became bishop of Salisbury. Stanley Katz points out that Harison "was at least partially in error once again. The letter . . . was ordered to be burned on January 21–23, 1693 by the House of Commons, not the Lords." Stanley N. Katz, ed., *A Brief Narrative of the Case and Trial of John Peter Zenger: Printer of the New York Weekly Journal, by James Alexander,* 2nd ed. (Cambridge, Mass.: Harvard University Press, 1972), 37, 225 n. 12. In 1689, Burnet had written to his diocesan clergy urging the pastors to take the oath of abjuration, renouncing any right of King James II to the throne. This was essentially a test oath for Englishmen to show their loyalty to King William and Queen Mary in the wake of the Glorious Revolution. Gilbert Burnet, *Bishop Burnet's History of His Own Time* (London: William Smith, 1840), 2:550. In 1693, by a vote of 169 to 155, the House of Commons ordered the letter burned because, according to a slim majority in the House, the letter threatened the church and the monarchy. More likely, as the English historian Thomas Macaulay noted, Burnet's "faults had made

for an Answer or promising to bring his Books, and did not return sitting the Court.

After Mr. Recorder's Departure, it was moved that the *Protest* should be entered; to which it was answered, That the *Protest* could not be entered without entering also the ORDER, and it was not fit to take any notice of IT, and therefore it was proposed that no Notice should be taken in their Books of either, which was unanimously agreed to by the Court.

The Sherriff then moved, that the Court would direct their Whipper to perform the said ORDER; to which it was answered, That as he was the Officer of the Corporation,[15] they would give no such *Order.* Soon after which the Court adjourned, and did not attend the Burning of the Papers. Afterwards about Noon, the Sheriff after reading the Numbers of the several Papers which were ordered to be burnt, delivered them unto the Hands of his own Negroe, and ordered him to put them into the Fire which he did, at which Mr. Recorder, *Jeremiah Dunbar,* Esq; and several of the Officers of the Garrison attended.[16]

Zenger's Arrest and His Lawyers' Disbarment

The Narrative *next recounts Zenger's arrest and the subsequent bail proceedings, after which it details the exceptions presented by Zenger's attorneys to the commissions of Chief Justice De Lancey and Justice Frederick Philipse. De Lancey responds to these challenges by disbarring Zenger's attorneys, James Alexander and William Smith, thus excluding them from practicing law in his court or anywhere in New York. On what basis did Alexander and Smith take exception to the validity of the judges' commissions? How might the attack on the justices' commissions have benefited Zenger?*

On the Lord's Day the *17th of November, 1734,* I was taken and imprisoned by Virtue of a Warrant in these Words.

---

him many enemies, and his virtues many more." Thomas B. Macaulay, *The History of England from the Accession of James II* (Philadelphia: Porter & Coates, 1876), 4:423–25.

[15]"Corporation" here refers to the city of New York. English cities, as well as those in the colonies, were created by corporate charters, usually granted by the king. To this day, New York remains a "municipal corporation," as do many other cities.

[16]Dunbar appears to be an obscure and historically unimportant supporter of Cosby.

At a Council held at Fort *George* in *New-York*, the *2d* Day of *November, 1734.*

PRESENT,

His Excellency *William Cosby,* Captain General and Governour in Chief, &c.

Mr. *Clarke.*	Mr. *Kennedy.*	Mr. *Lane.*
Mr. *Harison.*	Chief Justice.	Mr. *Horsmanden.*
Mr. *Livingston.*	Mr. *Cortlandt.*	

It is ordered that the Sheriff for the City of *New-York,* do forthwith take and apprehend *John Peter Zenger,* for printing and publishing several Seditious Libels, dispersed throughout his Journals or News Papers, entituled *The New-York Weekly Journal, containing the freshest Advices, foreign and domestick*; as having in them many Things, tending to raise Factions and Tumults, among the People of this Province, inflaming their Minds with Contempt of His Majesty's Government, and greatly disturbing the Peace thereof, and upon his taking the said *John Peter Zenger, to commit him to the Prison or common Goal of the said City and County.*

Fred. Morris, *D. Cl. Con.*

And being by Virtue of that Warrant so imprisoned in the Goal, I was for several Days denied the use of Pen, Ink and paper, and the Liberty of Speech with any Persons. — Upon my Commitment, some Friends soon got a *Habeas Corpus,* to bring me before the Chief Justice, in order to my Discharge, or being bailed; on the Return whereof, on *Wednesday* the *20th* of *November,* my Council[17] delivered Exceptions to the Return, and the Chief Justice ordered them to be argued publickly at the City-Hall, on the *Saturday* following.

On *Saturday* the *23d* of *November,* the said Exceptions came to be argued, by *James Alexander* and *William Smith,* of Council for me, and by Mr. Attorney General and Mr. *Warrel,*[18] of Council against me, in Presence of some Hundreds of the Inhabitants; where my Council (saving the Benefit of Exception to the illegality of the Warrant) insisted that I might be admitted to reasonable Bail. And to shew that it was my Right to be so, they offered *Magna Charta, The Petition of Right,* 3 Car. *The*

[17] This is the eighteenth-century spelling of the modern word *counsel,* which is another term for a lawyer.

[18] The attorney general was Richard Bradley, who had held that position since 1722. Warrel, or Worrell as it is usually spelled, was a minor lawyer notorious for his willingness to do Cosby's bidding and dirty work.

Habeas Corpus *Act of* 31 Car. 2. which directs the Sum in which Bail is to be taken, to be, *"according to the Quality of the Prisoner, and Nature of the Offence."* Also *2d Hawkins,* Cap. 15 §. 5, in these Words, *"But Justice must take Care, that under Pretence of demanding sufficient Security, they do not make so excessive a Demand, as in Effect amounts to a Denyal of Bail; for this is lookt on as a great Grievance, and is complained of as such,* by 1 W. & M. Sefs. 2d. *by which it is declared,* That excessive Bail ought not to be required." It was also shewn that the seven Bishops, who in King *James* the *IId's* Time, were charged with the like Crime that I stood charged with, were admitted to Bail on their own Recognizances, the Arch-Bishop in 200£ & each of the other six in a 100£ apiece only.[19] Sundry other Authorities and Arguments were produced and insisted on by my Council, to prove my Right to be admitted to moderate Bail, and to such Bail as was in my Power to give; and sundry Parts of History they produced, to shew how much the requiring excessive Bail had been resented by Parliament. And in order to Enable the Court to judge what Surety was in my Power to Give, I made Affidavit, *That (my Debts paid) I was not worth Forty Pounds, (the Tools of my Trade and wearing Apparel excepted).*

Some warm Expressions (to say no worse of them) were dropt on this Occasion sufficiently known and resented by the Auditory, which for my Part I desire may be buried in Oblivion: Upon the whole it was *Ordered that I might be admitted to Bail, my self in 400£ with two Sureties, each in 200£ and that I should be remanded till I Gave it.* And as this was Ten Times more than was in my Power to counter-secure any Person in giving Bail for me, I conceived I could not ask any to become my Bail on these Terms; and therefore I returned to Goal, where I lay until *Tuesday* the *28th of January, 173[5],* being the last Day of that Term; and the Grand Jury having found nothing against me, I Expected to have been discharged from my Imprisonment: But my Hopes proved vain; for the Attorney General then charged me by *Information,*[20] for

---

[19]The reference here is to *The Trial of the Seven Bishops,* 12 Howell's State Trials 183 (1688), which involved the prosecution for libel of seven of the bishops of the Church of England who had allegedly published a petition that challenged the authority of King James II. The bishops denied that they had published the libelous paper and, despite evidence pointing to their guilt, the jury acquitted them. Shortly thereafter, the Glorious Revolution erupted, leading to the overthrow of King James II.

[20]An information is like an indictment, except that it is brought by a prosecutor rather than a grand jury. Informations under common law were always limited to misdemeanors and could not be used to try someone for a felony. Trial by information was generally seen as arbitrary, even tyrannical, since it allowed the government to try people without first submitting the case to a grand jury. In Zenger's case, the grand jury refused to indict him.

Printing and publishing Parts, of my Journals No. 13 and 23, as being *false, scandalous, malicious and seditious.*[21]

To this Information my Council appeared, and offered Exceptions, leaving a Blank for inserting the Judges Commissions, which the Court were of opinion not to receive till those Blanks were filled up. In the succeeding Vacation the Judges gave Copies of their Commissions; and on *Tuesday* the *15th* of *April* last, the first Day of the succeeding Term, my Council offered these Exceptions; which were as follows.

> The Attorney General,
> *v.*
> *John Peter Zenger.*
> }
> On Information for a
> Misdemeanour.

Exceptions humbly offered by *John Peter Zenger*, to the Honourable *James De Lancey*, Esq; to judge in this Cause.

The Defendant comes and prays Hearing of the Commission, by Virtue of which the Honourable *James De Lancey*, Esq; claims the Power and Authority to judge in this Cause, and it is read to him in these Words;

GEORGE *the second, by the Grace of God, of* Great Britain, France *and* Ireland, *King, Defender of the Faith, &c. To Our trusty and well beloved* James De Lancey, *Esq; We reposing Special Trust and Confidence in your Integrity, Ability and Learning; have assigned, constituted and appointed, and We do by these Presents assign constitute and appoint you the said* James De Lancey, *to be Chief Justice in and over Our Province* of New-York, *in* America, *in the Room of* Lewis Morris, *Esq; Giving and by these Presents granting unto you, full Power and lawful Authority, to hear try and determine all Pleas whatsoever, civil, criminal and mixt, according to the Laws, Statutes and Customs of Our Kingdom of* England, *and the Laws and Usages, of Our said Province of* New-York, *not being repugnant thereto; and Executions of all Judgments of the said Court to award, and to make such Rules and Orders in the said Court, as may be found convenient and useful, and as near as may be, agreeable to the Rules and Orders of Our Courts of King's Bench, Common Pleas and Exchequer in* England. *To have hold and enjoy the said Office or Place of Chief Justice, in and over Our said Province, with all and singular the Rights, Privileges, Profits and Advantages, Sallaries, Fees and Perquisites unto the said Place belonging, or in any Ways appertaining, in as full and ample Manner*

---

[21]See Document 3 on page 132.

*as any Person heretofore Chief Justice of Our said Province hath held
and enjoyed, or of Right ought to have held and enjoyed the same, To
you the said* James De Lancey, *Esq; for and* DURING OUR WILL
AND PLEASURE. *In Testimony whereof we have caused these Our
Letters to be made Patent, and the great Seal of Our Province of* New-
York *to be hereunto affixed. Witness Our trusty and well beloved*
WILLIAM COSBY, *Esq; Our Captain General and Governour in
Chief of Our Provinces of* New-York, New-Jersey *and the Territories
thereon depending in* America, *Vice-Admiral of the same, and Colonel
in Our Army, at Fort* George, *in* New-York, *the Twenty-first day of*
August, *in the seventh Year of Our Reign,* Annoq; Domini, 1733.

Which being read and heard, the said *John Peter Zenger,* by
Protestation not confessing nor submitting to the Power of any
other Person to Judge in this Cause, doth except to the Power of the
Honourable *James De Lancey,* Esq; aforesaid to judge in this Cause,
by Virtue of the Commission aforesaid, for these Reasons, viz.

1st. For that the Authority of a Judge of the King's Bench, in that
Part of *Great Britain* called *England,* by which the Cognizance of
this Cause is claimed, is by the said Commission granted to the
Honourable *James De Lancey,* Esq; aforesaid, only *during Pleasure;*
whereas that Authority (by a Statute in that Case made and provided,) ought to be granted *during good Behaviour.*

2d. For that by the said Commission, the Jurisdiction and Authority of a Justice of the Court of Common Pleas at *Westminster* in that
Part of *Great-Britain,* called *England,* is granted to the said *James
De Lancey,* Esq; which Jurisdiction and Authority, cannot be granted
to, and exercised by, any one of the Justices of the King's Bench.

3d. For that the Form of the said Commission, is not founded on
nor warranted by the Common Law, nor any statute of *England,* nor
of *Great-Britain,* nor any Act of Assembly of this Colony.

4th. For that it appears by the Commission aforesaid, that the
same is granted under the Seal of this Colony, by His Excellency
William Cosby, Esq; Governour thereof; and it appears not, that the
same was granted, neither was the same granted, by and with the
Advice and Consent of His Majesty's Council of this Colony; without
which Advice and Consent, His Excellency could not grant the same.

Wherefore, and for many other Defects in the said Commission,
this Defendant humbly hopes, that the Honourable *James De Lancey*
Esq; will not take Cognizance of this Cause by Virtue of the Commission aforesaid.

Was signed,   {   *James Alexander.*
                      William Smith.

The Exceptions to the Commission of the Honourable *Frederick Philipse,* Esq; were the same with the foregoing, including therein his Commission, which is in these Words.

GEORGE *the second, by the Grace of God, of* Great Britain, France *and* Ireland, *King Defender of the Faith,* &c. *To Our trusty and well beloved* Frederick Philipse, *Esq; Greeting: Whereas it is Our Care, that Justice be duely administered to Our Subjects within Our Province of* New-York, *and Territories thereon depending in* America; *and We reposing especial Confidence, in your Integrity, Ability and Learning, have assigned, constituted and appointed, and We do by these Presents assign, constitute and appoint you the said* Frederick Philipse, *to be Second Justice, of Our Supream Court of Judicature of Our Province of* New-York, *in the Room of* James De Lancey, *Esq; Giving and granting unto you the said* Frederick Philipse, *full Power and Authority, with Our other Justices of Our said Supream Court, to hear, try and determine, all Ideas whatsoever, civil, criminal and mixt, according to the Laws, Statutes and Customs of Our Kingdom of* England, *and the Laws and Usages of Our said Province of* New-York, *not being repugnant thereto, and Executions of all Judgments of the said Court to award, and to act and do all Things, which any of Our* Justices of either Bench, or Baron of the Exchequer, in Our said Kingdom of *England, may or ought to do; and also to assist, in the making such Rules and Orders in Our said Court, as shall be for the Good and Benefit of Our said Province; and as near as conveniently may be, to the Rules and Orders of Our said Courts in Our said Kingdom of* England: *To have, hold and enjoy, the said Office or Place of Second Justice of our said Province of* New-York, *together with all and singular the Rights, Privileges, Salaries, Fees, Perquisites, Profits and Advantages thereto, now or at any Time heretofore belonging, or in any wise of Right appertaining; unto you the said* Frederick Philipse, *for and* during Our Pleasure. *In Testimony whereof, We have caused these our Letters to be made Patent, and the Great Seal of Our said Province of* New-York *to be hereunto affixed. Witness Our trusty and well beloved* WILLIAM COSBY, *Esq; Our Captain General and Governour in Chief, of Our Provinces of* New-York, New-Jersey, *and Territories thereon depending in* America, *Vice Admiral of the same, and Colonel in Our Army,* &c. *at* Fort George *in* New-York, *the Twenty-first*

Day of August, *in the Seventh Year of Our Reign,* Annoq; Domini, 1733.

Fred. Morris, D. Secry.

Tuesday, the *15th of April, 1735.*

Mr. *Alexander* offered the above Exceptions to the Court, and prayed that they might be filed. Upon this the Chief Justice said to Mr. *Alexander* and Mr. *Smith,* That they ought well to consider the Consequences of what they offered; to which both answered, That they had well considered what they offered, and all the Consequences. And Mr. *Smith* added, that he was so well satisfied of *the Right of the Subject to take an Exception to the Commission of a Judge, if he thought such Commission illegal,* —that he durst venture his Life upon *that Point.* As to *the Validity of the Exceptions* then offered, he said he took that to be a *second Point;* but was ready to argue them both, if their Honours were pleased to hear him. To which the Chief Justice replied, That he would consider the Exceptions in the Morning; and ordered the Clerk to bring them to him.

Wednesday the *16th April, 1735.*

The Chief Justice delivered one of the Exceptions to the Clerk, and Justice *Philipse* the other, upon which Mr. *Smith* arose and asked the Judges, whether Honours would hear him upon these two points.[22] *1st. That the Subject has a Right to take such Exceptions, if they judged the Commissions illegal. 2dly, That the Exceptions tendred were legal and valid.* To which the Chief Justice said, that they would neither hear nor allow the Exceptions; *for* (said he) *you thought to have gained a great Deal of Applause and Popularity by opposing this Court, as you did the Court of Exchequer; but you have brought it to that Point, That either,* We must go from the Bench, or you from the Barr: *Therefore We exclude you and Mr.* Alexander *from the Barr;* and delivered a Paper to the Clerk, and ordered it be entered, which the Clerk entered accordingly, and returned the Paper to the Chief Justice; after which the Chief Justice ordered the Clerk to read publickly what he had written; an attested Copy whereof follows.

---

[22] *This first point is largely treated on, in the Arguments of* Van Dam's *Council, in support of their Plea to the Jurisdiction of the Supream Court, printed here above a Year before that, from* Pag. *14 to 35, to which no Answer has as yet appeared; which Argument, contains also some Part of the Arguments necessary to support the 2d. Point.* [Zenger] [This is a reference to the pamphlets cited at note 10 of the Introduction.]

At a Supream Court of Judicature held for the Province of New-York, at the City Hall of the City of *New-York,* on *Wednesday,* the *16th* Day of *April,* 1735.

PRESENT,

The Honourable *James De Lancey,* Esq; Chief Justice.
The Honourable *Frederick Philipse,* Esq; Second Justice.

James Alexander, *Esq, and* William Smith, *Attornies of this Court, having presumed* (notwithstanding they were forewarned by the Court of their DISPLEASURE if they should do it) *to sign, and having actually signed, and put into Court, Exceptions in the Name of* John Peter Zenger; *thereby denying the Legality of the Judges their Commissions; tho' in the usual Form,*[23] and the being of this Supream Court. *It is therefore ordered, that for the said Contempt, the said* James Alexander, *and* William Smith, *be excluded from any farther Practice in this Court, and that their Names be struck out of the Roll of Attornies of this Court.*

per. Cur'.[24] James Lyne, *Cl.*

After the Order of the Court was read, Mr. *Alexander* asked whether it was the Order of Mr. Justice *Philipse* as well as of the Chief Justice? To which both answered, that it was their Order; upon which Mr. *Alexander* added, That it was proper to ask that Question, *That they might know how to have their Relief:* He farther observed to the Court, upon reading of the Order, That they were mistaken in their Wording of it, because the Exceptions were *only to their Commissions,* and *not to the being of the Court,* as is therein alledged; and prayed that the Order might be altered accordingly. The Chief Justice said, they conceived the Exceptions were against the Being of the Court. Both Mr. *Alexander* and Mr. *Smith* denied that they were, and prayed the Chief Justice to point to the Place that contained such Exception; and further added; That the Court might well exist, tho' the Commissions of all the Judges were void; which the Chief Justice confessed to be true: And therefore they prayed again that the Order in that Point might be altered; but it was denied.

Then Mr. *Alexander* desired to know, whether they *over ruled* or *rejected* the Exceptions; the Chief Justice said, he did not understand

---

[23] Of course, Alexander and Smith argued that the commissions were not in the "usual Form."

[24] Per curiam, or "by the court."

the Difference; to which said *Alexander* replied, that if he *rejected* the Exceptions, then they could not appear upon the Proceedings, and in that Case the Defendant was entitled to have them made Part of the Proceedings, by Bill of Exceptions: But if they *over ruled* them, then by so doing, they only declared them not sufficient, to hinder them from proceeding by virtue of those Commissions, and the Exceptions would remain as Records of the Court, and ought to be entered on the Record of the Cause as Part of the Proceedings. The Chief Justice said, they must remain upon the File, to warrant what we have done; as to being Part of the Record of the Proceedings in that Cause, he said, you may speak to that Point to morrow.

Fryday, April 18th, 1735.

Mr. *Alexander* signified to the Court, That on *Wednesday* last their Honours had said, That the Council for *Zenger* might speak to the Point, concerning the *Rejecting* or *Over ruling* of *Zenger's* Exceptions on the Morrow: To which the Chief Justice answered. That he said, *You may get some Person to speak to that Point on the Morrow, not meaning that the said* Alexander *should speak to it, that being contrary to the Order,* both Mr. *Alexander* and Mr. *Smith* said, they understood it otherwise.

They both also mentioned, that it was a Doubt, whether by the Words of the Order they were debarred of their Practice as Council, as well as Attornies, whereas they practiced in both Capacities?[25] To which the Chief Justice answered, That the Order was plain, *That* James Alexander, *Esq; and* William Smith, *were debarred and excluded from their whole Practice at this Barr, and that the Order was intended to barr their acting both as Council and as Attornies, and that it could not be construed otherwise,* And it being asked Mr. *Philipse,* whether he understood the Order so; he answered, that he did.

---

[25]The distinction here is between arguing the case before a court as a counselor at law and acting as an attorney to represent someone in business matters and real estate transactions. According to one early law dictionary, an "attorney at law" is "an officer in a court of justice, who is employed by a party in a cause to manage the same for him, as his advocate." The role of the attorney "is to carry on the practical and more mechanical parts of the suit." A "counsellor at law" is "employed by a party in a cause, to conduct the same on its trial on his behalf." The "duty of the counsel" is "to draft or review and correct the special pleadings, to manage the cause on trial, and during the whole course of the suit, to apply established principles of law to the exigencies of the case." John Bouvier, *A Law Dictionary Adapted to the Constitution and Laws of the United States of America* (Philadelphia: T. & J. W. Johnson, 1839), 1:104, 245.

A New Lawyer Prevents a Stacked Jury

His attorneys having been disbarred, Zenger asks the court to appoint a new lawyer to represent him. The court complies by appointing John Chambers, who is a supporter of Governor Cosby. This segment of the Narrative takes us to the start of the trial, explaining how Chambers took action to prevent first the court clerk and then the sheriff from stacking the jury with Cosby's friends and supporters. What strategies did the clerk and the sheriff employ in attempting to influence the jury selection? Is it likely that they were acting on their own initiative, or would it be more likely that Governor Cosby was "pulling the strings"? Why does Chambers, who is connected to the Cosby administration, offer such a strong defense of Zenger?

Upon this Exclusion of my Council I petitioned the Court to order Council for my Defence, who thereon appointed *John Chambers,* Esq;[26] who pleaded *Not Guilty* for me to the Information. But as to the Point. *Whether my Exceptions should be part of the Record as was moved by my former Council,* Mr. *Chambers* thought not proper to speak to it; Mr. *Chambers* also moved, that a certain Day in the next Term, might be appointed for my Tryal, and for *a Struck Jury;*[27] whereupon my Tryal was ordered to be on *Monday,* the *4th* of *August,* and the Court would consider till the first Day of next Term, whether I should have a Struck Jury or not, and ordered that the Sheriff should in the mean Time, at my Charge, return the Freeholders Book.[28]

At a Supream Court of Judicature held for the Province of *New-York,* before the Honourable *James De Lancey,* Esq; Chief Justice of the said Province; and The Honourable *Frederick Philipse,* Esq; second Justice of the said Province.

---

[26]Zenger, of course, had no "right to counsel" as modern Americans do. However, it would have been a political mistake for De Lancey to disbar Zenger's attorneys and not provide Zenger with some legal counsel.

[27]A "struck jury" was chosen in the following manner. A pool of jurors—usually forty-eight—was presented to counsel for both sides in a case. Each side alternately struck off one person from the panel until the panel was reduced to twelve members. These twelve people then constituted the jury. This procedure was usually reserved for unusual, important, or particularly complicated cases.

[28]The freeholders book contained the names of all adult male taxpayers who could serve as jurors.

On *Tuesday* the 29*th* of *July, 1735.* The Court opened, and *on Motion of Mr.* Chambers *for a Struck Jury, pursuant to the Rule of the preceding Term, the Court were of Opinion that I was entitled to have a Struck Jury;* and that Evening at five of the Clock, some of my Friends attended the Clerk, for striking the Jury; when to their Surprize, the Clerk instead of producing the Freeholders Book, to Strike the Jury of it in their Presence as usual, he produced a List of 48 Persons, who, he said he had taken out of the Freeholders Book; my Friends told him, that a great Number of these Persons were not Freeholders, that others were Persons holding Commissions and Offices at the Governour's Pleasure, that others were of the late displaced Magistrates of this City, who must be supposed to have Resentment against me, for what I had printed concerning them; that others were the Governour's Baker, Taylor, Shoemaker, Candlemaker, Joiner, &c. that as to the few indifferent Men that were upon that List, they had Reason to believe (as they had heard) that Mr. Attorney had a List of them, to strike them out; and therefore requested that he would either bring the Freeholders Book, and chuse out of it 48 unexceptionable Men in their Presence, as usual or else, that he would hear their Objections particularly to the List he offered, and that he would put impartial Men in the Place of those against whom they could shew just Objections. Notwithstanding this, the Clerk refused to strike the Jury out of the Freeholders Book, and refused to hear any Objections to the Persons on his List; but told my Friends, if any Objections they had to any Persons, they might strike those Persons out; to which they answered, there would not remain a Jury, if they struck out all the exceptionable Men, and according to the Custom, they had only a Right to strike out 12.

But finding no Arguments could prevail with the Clerk to hear their Objections to his List, nor to strike the Jury as usual, Mr. *Chambers* told him, he must apply to the Court, which the next Morning he did, and the Court upon his Motion *Ordered, That the 48 should be struck out of the Freeholders Book as usual, in the presence of the Parties, and that the Clerk should hear Objections to Persons proposed to be of the 48, and allow of such Exceptions as were just.* In Pursuance of that Order, a Jury was that Evening struck, to the Satisfaction of both Parties, [tho'] my Friends and Council insisted on no Objections but *want of* [Freehold]; and tho' they did not insist, that Mr. Attorney General (who was assisted by Mr. *Blagge,*)[29] should shew any particular Cause, against any Persons

---

[29] Edward Blagge was another lawyer associated with Cosby and, like Harison, particularly despised by the Morrisites for his corruption and venality.

he disliked, but acquiesced that *any person he disliked* should be [left] out of the 48.

Before *James De Lancey,* Esq; Chief Justice of the Province of *New-York,* and *Frederick Philipse,* second Judge, came on my Tryal, on the fourth Day of *August, 1735,* upon an Information for printing and publishing two News Papers, which were called Libels against our Governour and his Administration.

The Defendant *John Peter Zenger* being called appeared.

And the Sherrif returned his *Venire*[30] for the Tryal of the said Cause.

MR. CHAMBERS, OF COUNCIL FOR THE DEFENDANT. I humbly move Your Honours, that we may have Justice done by the Sherrif, and that he may return the Names of the Jurors in the same Order as they were struck.

CHIEF JUSTICE. *How is that? Are they not so returned?*

MR. CHAMBERS. No they are not: For some of the Names that were last set down in the Pannel, are now placed first.

CHIEF JUSTICE. *Make out that, and you shall be righted.*

MR. CHAMBERS. I have the Copy of the Pannel in my Hand, as the Jurors were struck, and if the Clerk will produce the Original signed by Mr. Attorney and my self, Your Honour will see our Complaint is just.

CHIEF JUSTICE. *Clerk, is it so? Look upon that Copy; is it a true Copy of the Pannel as it was struck?*

CLERK. Yes, I believe it is.

CHIEF JUSTICE. *How came the Names of the Jurors to be misplaced in the Pannel annexed to the* Venire?

SHERIFF. I have returned the Jurors in the same Order in which the Clerk gave them to me.

CHIEF JUSTICE. *Let the Names of the Jurors be ranged in the Order they were struck, agreeable to the Copy here in Court.*

Which was done accordingly. And the Jury, whose Names were as follows, were called and sworn.[31]

Harmanus Rutgers,	*Samuel Weaver,*	*Benjamin Hildreth,*
Stanly Holmes,	*Andries Marschalk,*	*Abraham Keteltas,*

[30] A *venire* is a writ to summon jurors to hear a trial. In this context, the author means that the sheriff returned his list of potential jurors.

[31] Significantly, half of the jurors were of Dutch ancestry and were probably likely to be particularly supportive of Zenger and his Dutch patron, Rip Van Dam. Historians have identified six of the jurors, including the foreman, Thomas Hunt, as men with ties to the Morrisite faction. Katz, *Brief Narrative,* 21–22.

| *Edward Man,* | *Egbert van Borsom,* | *John Goelet,* |
| *John Bell,* | *Thomas Hunt, Form.* | *Hercules Wendover.* |

The Charges against Zenger

This portion of the Narrative *presents the details of the information, or charge, against Zenger by New York attorney general Richard Bradley, who reads the information aloud to the court at the outset of the trial. The* Narrative *includes an extensive transcript of Bradley's opening remarks while offering only a brief summation of Chambers's response. What is the effect of the quotations from Zenger's paper that Bradley includes in his information? How does Bradley use language in an attempt to influence or manipulate the jury in his favor?*

Mr. Attorney General opened the Information, which was as follows.

MR. ATTORNEY. May it please Your Honours, and you Gentlemen of the Jury; the Information now before the Court, and to which the Defendant *Zenger* has pleaded *Not Guilty,* is an Information for printing and publishing *a false, scandalous, and seditious Libel,* in which His Excellency the Governour of this Province, who is the King's immediate Representative here, is greatly and unjustly scandalized, as a Person that has no Regard to Law nor Justice; with much more, as will appear upon reading the Information. This of Libelling is what has always been discouraged as a Thing that tends to create Differences among Men, ill Blood among the People, and oftentimes great Bloodshed between the Party Libelling and the Party Libelled. There can be no Doubt but you Gentlemen of the Jury will have the same ill opinion of such practices, as the judges have always shewn upon such Occasions: But I shall say no more at this Time, untill you hear the Information, which is as follows.

New-York, Supream Court.

of the Term of *January,* in the Eighth Year of the Reign of our Sovereign Lord King GEORGE the second, &c.
 New-York, Ss. BE it remembered, That *Richard Bradly,* Esq: Attorney General of Our Sovereign Lord the King, for the Province of *New-York,* who for Our said Lord the King in this Part prosecutes, in his own proper Person comes here into the Court of our said

Lord the King, and for our said Lord the King gives the Court here
to understand and be informed, That *John Peter Zenger,* late of the
City of *New-York,* Printer, (being a seditious Person; and a frequent
Printer and Publisher of false News and seditious Libels, and wick-
edly and maliciously devising the Government of Our said Lord the
King of this His Majesty's Province of *New-York,* under the Admin-
istration of His Excellency *William Cosby,* Esq; Captain General and
Governour, in Chief of the said Province, to traduce, scandalize and
vilify, and His Excellency the said Governour, and the Ministers and
Officers of Our said Lord, the King of and for the said Province to
bring into Suspicion and the ill Opinion of the Subjects of Our said
Lord the King residing within the Province) the Twenty eighth Day
of *January,* in the seventh Year of the Reign of Our Sovereign Lord
George the second, by the Grace of God of *Great-Britain, France* and
Ireland, King Defender of the Faith, &c. at the City of *New-York, did
falsly, seditiously and scandalously* print and publish, and cause to be
printed and published, a certain *false, malicious, seditious scandalous*
Libel, entitled *The New-York Weekly Journal, containing the freshest
Advices, foreign and domestick*; in which Libel (of and concerning
His excellency the said Governour, and the Ministers and Officers
of Our said Lord the king, of and for the said Province) among other
Things therein contained are these Words; *"Your Appearance in
Print at last,* gives a Pleasure to many, tho' most wish you had come
fairly into the open Field, and not appeared behind *Retrenchments*
made of the supposed Laws against Libelling, and of what other
Men have said and done before; these *Retrenchments,* Gentlemen,
may soon be shewn to you and all Men to be weak, and to have
neither Law nor Reason for their Foundation, so cannot long stand
you in stead: Therefore, you had much better as yet leave them, and
come to what *the People of this City and Province* (the City and
Province of *New-York* meaning) think are the Points in Question (*to
witt*) They (the People of the City and Province of *New-York* meaning) *think as Matters now stand, that their* LIBERTIES *and* PROP-
ERTIES *are precarious, and that* SLAVERY *is like to be intailed on
them and their Posterity, if some past Things be not amended, and
this they collect from many past Proceedings."* (Meaning many of the
past Proceedings of His Excellency the said Governour, and of the
Ministers and Officers of our said Lord the King, of and for the said
Province.) And [the said] Attorney General of Our said Lord the
King, for Our said Lord the King, likewise gives the Court here to
understand and be informed, that the said *John Peter Zenger* afterwards (*to wit*) the eighth Day of *April,* in the seventh Year of the

Reign of Our said Lord the King, at the City of *New-York* aforesaid, did *falsely, seditiously and scandalously* print and publish, and cause to be printed and published, another *false malicious seditious and scandalous* Libel, entituled, *the New-York Weekly Journal, containing the freshest Advices, foreign and domestic.* In which Libel, (of and concerning the Government of the said Province of *New-York*, and of and concerning His Excellency the said Governour, and the Ministers and Officers of Our said Lord the King, of and for the said Province) among other Things thercin contained, are these Words *"One of our Neighbours* (one of the Inhabitants of *New-Jersey* meaning) *being in Company, observing the Strangers* (some of the Inhabitants of *New-York* meaning) *full of Complaints, endeavoured to perswade them to remove into* Jersey; *to which it was replied, that would be leaping out of the Frying Pan into the Fire; for, says he, we both are under the same Governour* (His Excellency the said Governour meaning) *and your Assembly have shewn with a Witness what is to be expected from them; one that was then moving to* Pensilvania, (meaning one that was then removing from *New-York*, with intent to reside at *Pensilvania*) *to which Place it is reported several considerable Men are removing* (from *New-York* meaning) *expressed in Terms very moving, much Concern for the Circumstances of* New-York (the bad Circumstances of the Province and People of *New-York* meaning) *seemed to think them very much owing to the Influence that some Men* (whom he called *Tools*) *had in the Administration* (meaning the Administration of Government of the said Province of *New-York*) *said he was now going from them, and was not to be hurt by any Measures they should take, but could not help having some Concern for the Welfare of his Country-Men, and should be glad to hear that the Assembly* (meaning the General Assembly of the Province of *New-York*) *would exert themselves as became them, by shewing that they have the Interest of their Country more at Heart, than the Gratification of any private View of any of their Members, or being at all affected, by the Smiles or Frowns of a Governour,* (His Excellency the said Governour meaning) *both which ought equally to be despised, when the Interest of their Country is at stake. You says he, complain of the Lawyers, but I think the Law it self is at an End*, WE (the People of the Province of *New-York* meaning) SEE MENS DEEDS DESTROYED, JUDGES ARBITRARILY DISPLACED, NEW COURTS ERECTED WITHOUT CONSENT OF THE LEGISLATURE (within the Province of New-York meaning) BY WHICH IT SEEMS TO ME, TRIALS BY JURIES ARE TAKEN AWAY WHEN A GOVERNOUR PLEASES (His Excellency the said Governour meaning) MEN OF

KNOWN ESTATES DENYED THEIR VOTES, CONTRARY TO THE RECEIVED PRACTICE, THE BEST EXPOSITOR OF ANY LAW: *Who is then in that Province* (meaning the Province of *New-York,*) *that call* (can call meaning) *any Thing his own, or enjoy any Libery* (Liberty meaning) *longer than those in the Administration* (meaning the Administration of Government of the said Province of *New-York*) *will condescend to let them do it, for which Reason I have left it,* (the Province of *New-York* meaning) *as I believe more will.*" To the great Disturbance of the Peace of the said Province of *New-York*, to the Great Scandal of Our said Lord the King, of His Exceellency the said Governour, and of all others concerned in the Administration of the Government of the said Province, and against the Peace of Our Sovereign Lord the King His Crown and Dignity, &c. Whereupon the said Attorney General of Our said Lord the King, for Our said Lord the King, prays the Advisement of the Court here, in the Premises, and the due Process of the Law, against him the said *John Peter Zenger*, in this Part to be done, to answer to Our said Lord the King of and in the Premises, &c.

R. Bradley, Attorney General.

To this Information the Defendant has pleaded *Not Guilty*, and we are ready to prove it.

Mr. Chambers *has not been pleased to favour me with his Notes, so I cannot, for Fear of doing him Injustice, pretend to set down his Argument; But here Mr.* Chambers *set forth very clearly the Nature of a Libel, the great Allowances that ought to be made for what Men speak or write, That in all Libels there must be some particular Persons so clearly pointed out, that no Doubt must remain about who is meant; That he was in hopes* Mr. Attorney *would fail in his Proof, as to this Point; and therefore desired that he would go on to examine his Witnesses.*

A Second New Lawyer Surprises the Court and Confuses the Prosecutor

At this point, Andrew Hamilton, the most famous and most skilled attorney in the colonies, makes his first appearance in the courtroom and in the Narrative. *James Alexander had secretly contacted Hamilton, who lived in Philadelphia, and recruited him on Zenger's behalf. Hamilton's arrival took everyone by surprise and clearly unnerved Attorney General Bradley. After recounting Hamilton's opening statements to the court and his initial exchanges with the attorney general, the* Narrative *offers a detailed summation of Bradley's argument for finding Zenger guilty of seditious libel, followed by a very brief recap of Chambers's reply. What advantages did Hamilton and his client hope to obtain from Hamilton's unexpected entrance and from the content of his opening statements? How did Bradley's subsequent arguments address the proposition of Zenger's attorneys that the prosecution would have to prove the falsity of the newspaper articles in order to prove they were libelous?*

Then Mr. *Hamilton*, who at the Request of some of my Friends, was so kind as to come from *Philadelphia*, to assist me on the Tryal, spoke.

MR. HAMILTON. May it please your Honour; I am concerned in this Cause on the Part of Mr. *Zenger* the Defendant. The Information against my Client was sent me, a few Days before I left Home, with some Instructions to let me know how far I might rely upon the Truth of those Parts of the Papers set forth in the Information, and which are said to be libellous. And tho' I am perfectly of the Opinion with the Gentleman who has just now spoke, on the same Side with me, as to the common Course of Proceedings, I mean in putting Mr. Attorney upon proving, that my Client printed and published those Papers mentioned in the Information; yet I cannot think it proper for me (without doing Violence to my own Principles) to deny the Publication of a Complaint, which I think is the Right of every free-born Subject to make, when the Matters so published can be supported with Truth; and therefore I'll save Mr. Attorney the Trouble of Examining his Witnesses to that Point; and I do (for my Client) confess, that he both printed and published the two News Papers set forth in the Information, and I hope in so doing he has committed no Crime.

MR. ATTORNEY. Then if Your Honour pleases, since Mr. *Hamilton* has confessed the Fact, I think our Witnesses may be discharged; we have no further Occasion for them.

MR. HAMILTON. If you brought them here, only to prove the Printing and Publishing of these News Papers, we have acknowledged that, and shall abide by it.

Here my Journeyman and two Sons (with several others subpoena'd by Mr. Attorney, to give Evidence against me) were discharged, and there was Silence in the Court for some Time.

MR. CHIEF JUSTICE. *Well Mr. Attorney, will you proceed?*

MR. ATTORNEY. Indeed Sir, as Mr. *Hamilton* has confessed the Printing
and Publishing these Libels, I think the Jury must find a Verdict for
the King;³² for supposing they were true, the Law says that they are
not the less libellous for that; nay indeed the Law says, their being
true is an Aggravation of the Crime.
MR. HAMILTON. Not so neither, Mr. Attorney, there are two Words to that
Bargain. I hope it is not our bare Printing and Publishing a Paper, that
will make it a Libel: You will have something more to do, before you
make my Client a Libeller; for the Words themselves must be libellous, that is, *false, scandalous, and seditious* or else we are not guilty.

*As Mr. Attorney has not been pleased to favour us with his Argu-
ment, which he read, or with the Notes of it, we cannot take upon us to
set down his Words, but only to shew the Book Cases he cited, and the
general Scope of his Argument, which he drew from those Authorities.
He observed upon the Excellency, as well as Use of Government, and the
great Regard and Reverence, which had been constantly paid to it, both
under the Law and Gospel. That by Government we were protected in
our Lives, Religion and Properties; and that for these Reasons, great
Care had always been taken to prevent every Thing that might tend to
scandalize Magistrates, and others concerned in the Administration of
the Government, especially the supream Magistrate. And that there were
many Instances of very severe Judgments, and of Punishments inflicted
upon such, as had attempted to bring the Government into Contempt;
by publishing false and scurrilous Libels against it, or by speaking evil
and scandalous Words of Men in Authority; to the great Disturbance of
the publick Peace. And to support this, he cited 5 Coke 121, (suppose
it should be 125), Wood's Instit 430, 2 Lilly 168, 1 Hawkins 73. 11.6.³³
From these Books he insisted, that a Libel was a malicious Defamation of any Person, expressed either in Printing or Writing, Signs or
Pictures, to asperse the Reputation of one that is alive, or the Memory
of one that is dead; if he is a private Man, the Libeller deserves a severe
Punishment, but if it is against a Magistrate or other publick Person, it
is a greater Offence; for this concerns not only the Breach of the Peace,
but the Scandal of the Government; for what greater Scandal of Government can there be, than to have corrupt or wicked Magistrates to
be appointed by the King, to govern his Subjects under him? And a*

³²Bradley asks for a "Verdict for the King" because throughout the British Empire, prosecutions were always brought in the name of the monarch, in this case King George II.
³³These references are to *Coke's Reports*; Thomas Wood, *Institutes of the Laws of
England* (London, 1720); John Lilly, *Practical Register; or General Abridgment of the Law*
(London, 1719); and Hawkins, *Pleas of the Crown*.

greater Imputation to the State cannot be, than to suffer such corrupt Men to sit in the sacred Seat of Justice, or to have any Medling in, or concerning the Administration of Justice: And from the same Books Mr. Attorney insisted, that whether the Person defamed is a private Man or a Magistrate, whether living or Dead, whether the Libel is true or false, or if the Party against whom it is made is of good or evil Fame, it is nevertheless a Libel: For in a settled State of Government, the Party grieved ought to complain for every injury done him, in the ordinary Course of the Law. And as to its Publication, the Law had taken so great Care of Men's Reputations, that if one maliciously repeats it, or sings it in the Presence of an other, or delivers the Libel or a Copy of it over, to scandalize the Party, he is to be punished as a Publisher of a Libel. He said it was likewise evident, that Libelling was an Offence against the Law of God. Act. XXIII. 5.[34] "Then said *Paul,* I wist not Brethren, that he was the High Priest: For it is written, thou shalt not speak evil of the Ruler of the People." *2. Pet. X. II.*[35] "Despise Government, presumptuous are they, self willed, they are not afraid to speak evil of Dignities, &c." *He then insisted that it was clear, both by the Law [of] God and Man, That it was a very great Offence to speak evil of, or to revile those in Authority over us; and that Mr. Zenger had offended in a most notorious and gross Manner, in scandalizing His Excellency our Governour, who is the King's immediate Representative, and the Supream Magistrate of this Province: For can there be any Thing more scandalous said of a Governour, than what is published in those Papers? Nay, not only the Governour, but both the Council and Assembly are scandalized; for there it is plainly said, That* as Matters now stand, their Liberties and Properties are precarious, and that Slavery is like to be entailed on them and their Posterity. *And then again Mr.* Zenger *says,* The Assembly ought to despise the Smiles or Frowns of a Governour; That he thinks the Law is at an End; That we see Mens Deeds destroyed, Judges arbitrarily displaced, new Courts erected, without Consent of the Legislature; *And* That it seems Tryals by Juries are taken away when a Governour pleases; That none can call any Thing their own, longer than those in the Administration will condescend to let them do it....

---

[34] The reference is to the New Testament, Acts 22:5.

[35] The reference is to the New Testament, 2 Peter 2:11. This citation and the quotation, however, are incorrect; the quotation is actually from verse 10, which reads: "But chiefly them that walk after the flesh in the lust of uncleanness, and despise government. Presumptuous *are they,* self-willed, they are not afraid to speak evil of dignities." King James Version.

And Mr. Attorney added, that he did not know what could be said in Defence of a Man, that had so notoriously scandalized the Governour and principal Magistrates and Officers of the Government, by charging them with depriving the People of their Rights and Liberties, and taking away Tryals by Juries, and in short, putting an End to the Law itself.—If this was not a Libel, he said, he did not know what was one. Such Persons as will take those Liberties with Governours and Magistrates, he thought ought to suffer for stirring up Sedition and Discontent among the People. And concluded by saying, that the Government had been very much traduced and exposed by Mr. Zenger, *before he was taken Notice of; that at last it was the Opinion of the Governour and Council, that he ought not to be suffered to go on, to disturb the Peace of the Government; by publishing such Libels against the Governour, and the chief Persons in the Government; And therefore they had directed this Prosecution, to put a Stop to this scandalous and wicked Practice, of libelling and defaming His Majesty's Government and disturbing his Majesty's Peace.*

Mr. Chambers *then sum'd up to the Jury, observing with great Strength of Reason on Mr. Attorney's defect of Proof, that the Papers in the Information were* False, Malicious or Seditious, *which was incumbent on him to prove to the Jury, and without which they could not on their Oaths say,* That they were so, as charged.

Asserting Truth as a Defense

In this segment of the Narrative, *Hamilton begins to lay out his argument that truth should be allowed as a defense against a charge of libel. He begins by setting out the differences between England and its American colonies and between the king and one of his appointed officials—in this case, the governor of New York. How does Hamilton draw on the opinions and statements of justices in previous libel cases to build his argument that the prosecution's only task is to prove that the articles in Zenger's paper were false (an assertion that both Bradley and De Lancey take issue with)? How does he address the contention that the truth of a libel increases the seriousness of the offense?*

MR. HAMILTON. May it please Your Honour; I agree with Mr. Attorney, that Government is a sacred Thing, but I differ very widely from him when he would insinuate, that the just Complaints of a Number of Men, who suffer under a bad Administration, is libelling that Administration. Had I believed that to be Law, I should not have given the Court the Trouble of hearing any Thing that I could say in this Cause. I own, when I read the Information, I had not the Art to find out (without the Help of Mr. Attorney's *Innuendo's*) that the Governor was the Person meant in every Period of that News Paper; and I was inclined to believe, that they were wrote by some, who from an extraordinary Zeal for Liberty, had misconstrued the Conduct of some Persons in Authority into Crimes; and that Mr. Attorney out of his too great Zeal for Power, had exhibited this Information, to correct the Indiscretion of my Client; and at the same Time, to shew his Superiors the great Concern he had, lest they should be treated with any undue Freedom. But from what Mr. Attorney has just now said, *to wit,* That this Prosecution was directed by the Governor and Council, and from the Extraordinary Appearance of People of all Conditions, which I observe in Court upon this Occasion, I have Reason to think, that those in the Administration have by this Prosecution something more in View, and that the People believe they have a good deal more at stake, than I apprehended: And therefore, as it is become my Duty, to be both plain and particular in this Cause, I beg Leave to bespeak the Patience of the Court.

I was in hopes, as that terrible Court, where those dreadful Judgments were given, and that Law established, which Mr. Attorney has produced for Authorities to support this Cause, was long ago laid aside, as the most dangerous Court to the Liberties of the People of *England,* that ever was known in that Kingdom; that Mr. Attorney knowing this, would not have attempted to set up a Star-Chamber here,[36] nor to make their Judgments a Precedent to us: For it is well known, that what would have been judg'd Treason in those Days for a Man to speak, I think, has since not only been practiced as lawful, but the contrary Doctrine has been held to be Law.

---

[36]The Court of Star Chamber was a court used by English monarchs, especially King James I and King Charles I, to prosecute their political opponents. The court was notorious for its arbitrary procedures and rulings and its general disregard for due process. It operated without a jury and without normal English legal rules and used torture to coerce confessions and punish defendants. The Star Chamber came to be a symbol of judicial tyranny and arbitrary government. Though abolished in 1641, its precedents, especially those on seditious libel, were still good law at this time. Throughout his arguments, Andrew Hamilton keeps reminding the court, the jury, and the audience attending the trial that the refusal to allow truth as a defense or to allow a jury to decide the case came from the Star Chamber.

In *Brewster's* Case,[37] for Printing, *That the Subjects might defend their Rights and Liberties by Arms, in case the King should go about to destroy them,* he was told by the Chief Justice that it was a great Mercy, he was not proceeded against for his Life; for that to say, the King could be resisted by Arms in any Case whatsoever, was express Treason. And yet we see since that Time, Dr. *Sacheverell*[38] was sentenced in the highest Court in *Great Britain*, for saying, *That such a Resistance was not lawful.* Besides, as Times have made very great Changes in the Laws of *England*, so in my Opinion there is good Reason that Places should do so too.

Is it not surprizing to see a Subject, upon his receiving a Commission from the King to be a Governor of a Colony in *America*, immediately imagining himself to be vested with all the Prerogatives belonging to the sacred Person of his Prince? And which is yet more astonishing, to see that a People can be so wild as to allow of and acknowledge those Prerogatives and Exemptions, even to their own Destruction? Is it so hard a Matter to distinguish between the Majesty of our Sovereign, and the Power of a Governor of the Plantations? Is not this making very free with our Prince, to apply that Regard, Obedience and Allegiance to a Subject, which is due only to Our Sovereign? And yet in all the Cases which Mr. Attorney has cited, to shew the Duty and Obedience we owe to the Supreme Magistrate, it is the King that is there meant and understood, tho' Mr. Attorney is pleased to urge them as Authorities to prove the Heinousness of Mr. *Zenger's* Offence against the Governor of *New-York*. The several Plantations are compared to so many large Corporations,[39] and perhaps not improperly; and can anyone give an instance, that the Mayor or Head of a Corporation, ever put in a Claim to the sacred Rights of Majesty? Let us not (while we are pretending to pay a great Regard to our Prince and His Peace) make bold to transfer that Allegiance to a Subject, which we owe to our King only. What strange Doctrine is it, to press every Thing for Law here which is so in *England?* I Believe we should not think it a Favour, at present at least, to establish this Practice. In *England* so great a Regard and Reverence is had to the Judges,[40] that if any Man strikes another in *Westminster Hall,* while the Judges are sitting, he shall lose his Right Hand, and forfeit his

---

[37] *The Trials of . . . Thomas Brewster, Bookseller,* 6 Howell's State Trials 513 (1664).
[38] On Sacheverell, see note 13.
[39] The English often referred to the American colonies themselves as plantations.
[40] *C. 3 Inst.* 140. [Zenger] [The reference is to volume 3 of *Coke's Institutes* (1641), which was the most common text for legal education in the colonies.]

Land and Goods, for so doing. And tho' the Judges here claim all the Powers and Authorities within this Government, that a Court of King's Bench has in *England*, yet I believe Mr. Attorney will scarcely say, that such a Punishment could be legally inflicted on a Man for committing such an Offence, in the Presence of the Judges sitting in any Court within the Province of *New-York*. The Reason is obvious; a Quarrel or Riot in *New-York*, cannot possibly be attended with those dangerous Consequences that it might in *Westminister Hall*; nor (I hope) will it be alledged, that any Misbehaviour to a Governor in the Plantations will, or ought to be, judged of or punished, as a like Undutifulness would be, to Our Sovereign. From all which, I hope Mr. Attorney will not think it proper to apply his Law-Cases (to support the Cause of his Governor) which have only been judged, where the King's Safety or Honour was concerned. It will not be denied but that a Freeholder in the Province of *New-York*, has as good a Right to the sole and separate Use of his Lands, as a Freeholder in *England*, who has a Right to bring an Action of Trespass against his Neighbour, for suffering his Horse or Cow to come and feed upon his Land, or eat his Corn, whether inclosed or not inclused; and yet I believe it would be looked upon as a strange Attempt, for one Man here, to bring an Action against another, whose Cattle and Horses feed upon his Grounds not inclosed, or indeed for eating and treading down his Corn, if that were not inclosed.[41] Numberless are the Instances of this Kind that might be given, to shew, that what is good Law at one Time and in one Place, is not so at another Time and in another Place; so that I think, the Law seems to expect, that in these Parts of the World Men should take Care, by a good Fence, to preserve their Property, from the Injury of unruly Beasts. And perhaps there may be a good Reason why Men should take the same Care, to make an honest and upright Conduct [as] a Fence and Security against the Injury of unruly Tongues.

MR. ATTORNEY. I don't know what the Gentleman means, by comparing Cases of Freeholders in *England* with Freeholders here. What has this Case to do with Actions of Trespass, or Men's Fencing their Ground? The Case before the Court is, whether Mr. *Zenger* is guilty

---

[41] The reference here is to the differences between English common law and what was emerging as American common law. In England, no one was obligated to fence his or her land. Rather, the owner of an animal was obligated to prevent his or her cattle, horses, or sheep from wandering onto a neighbor's land. In America, however, the general rule was that a landowner was obligated to fence out animals and other trespassers. A New York act of 1734 set the height for stone fences (three feet eight inches) and wooden rail fences (four feet).

of Libelling His Excellency the Governor of *New-York*, and indeed the whole Administration of the Government? Mr. *Hamilton*, has confessed the Printing and Publishing, and I think nothing is plainer, than that the Words in the Information are *scandalous, and tend to sedition, and to disquiet the Minds of the People of this Province*. And if such Papers are not Libels, I think it may be said, there can be no such Thing as a Libel.

MR. HAMILTON. May it please Your Honour; I cannot agree with Mr. Attorney: For tho' I freely acknowledge, that there are such Things as Libels, yet I must insist at the same Time, that what my Client is charged with, is not a Libel; and I observed just now, that Mr. Attorney in defining a Libel, made use of the Words, *scandalous, seditious and tend to disquiet the People;* but (whether with Design or not I will not say) he omitted the Word *false*.

MR. ATTORNEY. I think I did not omit the Word *false*: But it has been said already, that it may be a Libel, notwithstanding it may be true.

MR. HAMILTON. In this I must still differ with Mr. Attorney; for I depend upon it, we are to be tried upon this Information now before the Court and Jury, and to which we have pleaded *Not Guilty*, and by it we are charged with Printing and publishing *a certain false, malicious, seditious and scandalous Libel*. This Word *false* must have some Meaning, or else how came it there? I hope Mr. Attorney will not say, he put it there by Chance, and I am of Opinion his Information would not be good without it. But to shew that it is the principal Thing which, in my Opinion, makes a Libel, I put the Case, [if] the Information had been for printing and publishing a certain *true* Libel, would that be the same Thing? Or could Mr. Attorney support such an Information by any Precedent in the *English* Law? No, the Falshood makes the Scandal, and both make the Libel. And to shew the Court that I am in good Earnest, and to save the Court's Time, and Mr. Attorney's Trouble, I will agree, that if he can prove the Facts charged upon us, to be *false*, I'll own them to be *scandalous, seditious* and *a Libel*. So the Work seems now to be pretty much shortned, and Mr. Attorney has now only to prove the Words false, in order to make us Guilty.

MR. ATTORNEY. We have nothing to prove; you have confessed the Printing and Publishing; but if it was necessary (as I insist it is not) how can we prove a Negative? But I hope some Regard will be had to the Authorities that have been produced, and that supposing all the Words to be true, yet that will not help them, that Chief Justice *Holt* in his Charge to the Jury, in the Case of *Tutchin*, made no Distinction, whether *Tutchin's* Paper's were *true* or *false;* and as Chief Justice *Holt* has made no Distinction in that Case, so none ought to be made here; nor can it be shewn in all that Case, there was any Question made about their being *false* or *true*.[42]

MR. HAMILTON. I did expect to hear, That a Negative cannot be proved; but every Body knows there are many Exceptions to that general Rule: For if a Man is charged with killing another, or stealing his Neighbour's Horse, if he is innocent, in the one Case, he may prove the Man said to be killed, to be really alive; and the Horse said to be stoln, never to have been out of his Master's Stable, &c. and this I think is proving a Negative. But we will save Mr. Attorney the Trouble of proving a Negative, and take the *Onus probandi*[43] upon our selves, and prove those very Papers that are called Libels to be *true*.

MR. CHIEF JUSTICE. You cannot be admitted, Mr. *Hamilton*, to give the Truth of a Libel in Evidence. A Libel is not to be justified; for it is nevertheless a Libel that it is *true*.

MR. HAMILTON. I am sorry the Court has so soon resolved upon that Piece of Law; I expected first to have been heard to that Point. I have not in all my Reading met with an Authority that says, we cannot be admitted to give the Truth in Evidence, upon an Information for a Libel.

MR. CHIEF JUSTICE. The Law is clear, That you cannot justify a Libel.

MR. HAMILTON. I own that, may it please Your Honour, to be so; but, with Submission, I understand the Word, *justify*, there, to be a justification by Plea, as it is in the Case upon an Indictment for *Murder*, or an *Assault and Battery*; there the Prisoner cannot justify, but plead *Not Guilty*: Yet it will not be denied but he may, and always is admitted, to give the Truth of the Fact, or any other Matter, in Evidence, which goes to his Acquital; as in Murder, he may prove it was in Defence of his Life, his House, &c. and in Assault and Battery, he may give in Evidence, that the other Party struck first, and in both Cases he will be acquitted. And in this Sense I understand the Word *justify*, when applied to the Case before the Court.

MR. CHIEF JUSTICE. I Pray shew that you can give the Truth of a Libel in Evidence.

MR. HAMILTON. I am ready, both from what I understand to be the Authorities in the Case, and from the Reason of the Thing, to shew that we may lawfully do so. But here I beg leave to observe, That Informations

---

[42] *The Trial of John Tutchin,* 14 Howell's State Trials 1095 (1704).
[43] Latin for "burden of proof."

for Libels is a Child, if not born, yet nursed up, and brought to full Maturity, in the Court of Star-Chamber.

MR. CHIEF JUSTICE. Mr. *Hamilton* you'll find your self mistaken; for in *Coke's Institutes* you'll find Informations for Libels, long before the Court of Star-Chamber.

MR. HAMILTON. I thank Your Honour; that is an Authority I did propose to speak to by and by: But as you have mention'd, it I'll read that Authority now. I think it is in *3 Co. Inst.* under Title *Libel*; it is the Case of *John de Northampton* for a Letter wrote to *Robert de Ferrers*, one of the King's privy Council,[44] concerning Sir *William Scot*, Chief Justice, and his Fellows; but it does not appear to have been upon Information; and I have good Grounds to say it was upon Indictment, as was the Case of *Adam de Ravensworth*, just mentioned before by Lord *Coke*, under the same Title; and I think there cannot be a greater, at least a plainer Authority for us, than the Judgment in the Case of *John de Northampton*, which my Lord has set down at large. *Et quia præ-dictus Johannes cognovit dictam Litteram per se scriptam Roberto de Ferrers, qui est de Concilio Regis, qua littera continet in senullam veri-tatem, &c.*[45] Now Sir, by this Judgment it appears the libelous Words were utterly false, and there the Falshood was the Crime, and is the Ground of that Judgment: And is not that what we contend for? Do not we insist that the Falshood makes the Scandal, and both make the Libel? And how shall it be known whether the Words are libelous, *that is, true* or *false*, but by admitting us to prove them *true*, since Mr. Attorney will not undertake to prove them *false*? Besides, is it not against common Sense, that a Man should be punished in the same Degree for a *true Libel* (if any such Thing could be) as for a *false one*? I know it is said, *That Truth makes a Libel the more provoking, and therefore the Offence is the greater, and consequently the Judgment should be the heavier.* Well, suppose it were so, and let us agree for once, *That Truth is a greater Sin than Falshood:* Yet as the Offences are not equal, and as the Punishment is arbitrary, *that is,* according as the Judges in their Discretion shall direct to be inflicted; is it not absolutely necessary that they should know, whether the Libel is *true* or *false*, that they may by that Means be able to proportion the Punishment? For, would it not be a sad Case, if the Judges, for want of a due Information, should chance to give as severe a Judgment against

---

[44] *Coke 3 Inst.* 174. [Zenger]
[45] The Latin roughly translates as "The aforementioned John admits he wrote the said letter, of Robert de Ferrers, of the King's council, and that the letter contains nothing that is true, etc."

a Man for writing or publishing a Lie, as for writing or publishing a Truth? And yet this (with submission) as monstrous and ridiculous as it may seem to be, is the natural Consequence of Mr. Attorney's Doctrine, *That Truth makes a worse Libel than Falshood*, and must follow from his not proving our Papers to be false, or not suffering us to prove them to be *true*. But this is only reasoning upon the Case, and I will now proceed to shew, what in my Opinion will be sufficient to induce the Court, to allow us to prove the Truth of the Words, which in the Information are called Libellous. And first, I think there cannot be a greater Authority for us, than the Judgment I just now mentioned, in the case of *John de Northampton*, and that was in early Times, and before the Star-Chamber came to its Fulness of Power and Wickedness. In that Judgment, as I observed, the *Falshood* of the Letter which was wrote, is assigned as the very Ground of the Sentence. And agreeable to this it was urged by Sir *Robert Sawyer*, in the Tryal of the Seven Bishops,[46] *That the Falsity, the Malice, and Sedition of the Writing, were all Facts to be proved*.[47] But here it may be said, Sir *Robert* was one of the Bishop's Council, and his Argument is not to be allowed for Law: But I offer it only to shew that we are not the first who have insisted, that to make a Writing a Libel, it must be *false*. And if the Argument of a Council must have no Weight, I hope there will be more Regard shewn to the Opinion of a Judge, and therefore I mention the Words of Justice *Powel* in the same Tryal, where he says (of the Petition of the Bishops, which was called a Libel, and upon which they were prosecuted by Information) That *to make it a Libel, it must be false and malicious, and tend to Sedition*; and declared, *as he saw no Falshood or Malice in it, he was of Opinion, that it was no Libel*. Now I should think this Opinion alone, in the Case of the King, and in a Case which that King had so much at Heart, and which to this Day has never been contradicted, might be a sufficient Authority, to entitle us to the Liberty of proving the *Truth* of the Papers, which in the Information are called *false, malicious, seditious and scandalous*. If it be objected, *that the Opinions of the other three Judges were against him*; I answer, That the Censures the Judgments of these Men have undergone, and the Approbation Justice *Powel's* Opinion, his Judgment and Conduct upon that Tryal has met with, and the Honour he gained to himself, for daring to speak Truth at such a Time, upon such an Occasion, and in the Reign of such a King,

---

[46] *State Tryals*, Vol. 4. [Zenger]
[47] See note 19 for a discussion of *The Trial of the Seven Bishops*.

is more than sufficient, in my humble Opinion, to warrant our insisting on his Judgment, as a full Authority to our Purpose; and it will lye upon Mr. Attorney to shew, that his Opinion has since that Time been denied to be Law, or that Justice *Powel* who delivered it, has ever been condemned or blamed for it, in any Law-Book extant at this Day, and this I will venture to say, Mr. Attorney cannot do. But to make this Point yet more clear, if any Thing can be clearer, I will on our Part proceed and shew, that in the Case of Sir *Samuel Barnardiston*, His Council, notwithstanding he stood before one of the greatest Monsters that ever presided in any *English* Court (Judge *Jefferies*) insisted on the Want of Proof, to the *Malice* and *seditious Intent* of the Author, of what was called a *Libel*.[48] And in the Case of *Tutchin*, which seems to be Mr. Attorney's chief Authority, that Case is against him; for he was, upon his Tryal put upon shewing the Truth of his Papers, but did not, at least the Prisoner was asked, by the King's Council, whether he would say they were *true*?[49] And as he never pretended, that they were true, the Chief Justice was not to say so. But the Point will still be clearer on our Side from *Fuller's* Case, *For falsly and wickedly causing to be printed a false and scandalous Libel, in which (amongst other Things) were contained these Words, "Mr. Jones has also made Oath, That he paid £5000 more, by the late King's Order, to several Persons in Places of Trust, that they might compleat my Ruin, and invalidate me forever. Nor is this all; for the same Mr. Jones will prove by undeniable Witness and Demonstration, that he has distributed more than £180,000, in Eight Years last past, by the French King's Order, to Persons in publick Trust in this Kingdom."*[50] Here you see is a scandalous and infamous Charge against the late King; here is a Charge no less than High Treason, against the *Men in publick Trust*, for receiving Money of the *French* King, then in actual War with the Crown of *Great Britain*; and yet the Court were far from bearing him down with that Star Chamber Doctrine, *to wit, That it was no matter, whether what he said was true or false*; no, on the contrary, Lord Chief Justice *Holt* asks *Fuller, "Can you make it appear, they are true? Have you any Witnesses? You might have had Subpoena's for your Witnesses against*

---

[48] *Case of Sir Samuel Barnardiston,* Court of King's Bench, 13 Howell's State Trials 845 (1684). The reference to Judge Jeffreys is important. Jeffreys, chief justice of the King's Bench, was notorious for his arbitrary and ruthless jurisprudence. In 1685, he ordered the hanging of more than three hundred men, earning the nickname "Bloody" Jeffreys.

[49] *State Trials* Vol. V, 549. [Zenger] [*Case of John Tutchin* (1704)]

[50] *State Trials* Vol. V, 445. [Zenger] [*Case of William Fuller* (1702)]

this Day. If you take upon you to write such Things as you are charged with, it lies upon you to prove them true, at your Peril. If you have any Witnesses, I will hear them. How came you to write those Books which are not true? If you have any Witnesses, produce them. If you can offer any Matter to prove what you have wrote, let us hear it. "Thus said, and thus did, that great Man Lord Chief Justice *Holt*, upon a Tryal of the like Kind with ours, and the Rule laid down by him in this Case is, *That he who will take upon him to write Things, it lies upon him to prove them, at his Peril.* Now, Sir, we have acknowledged the Printing and Publishing of those Papers, set forth in the Information, and (with the Leave of the Court) agreeable to the Rule laid down by Chief Justice *Holt*, we are ready to prove them to be true, at our Peril.

MR. CHIEF JUSTICE. Let me see the Book.

Here the Court had the Case under Consideration, a considerable Time, and every one was silent.

Hamilton's Appeal to the Jury

This section of the Narrative *recounts sharp exchanges between Hamilton and Chief Justice De Lancey regarding Hamilton's claims that English precedent supports using truth as a defense and allowing the jury to decide if the publications at issue were libelous. Hamilton spars with Bradley as well before embarking on a long soliloquy on a society's need for and right to free speech in order to combat abuses of power by government officials. By this point in the trial, it is clear that the older and more experienced Hamilton is able to make statements to the court—his attacks on the use of Court of Star Chamber precedents, for example—that might have led De Lancey to disbar a less important and less famous lawyer. Who has the better argument here, Hamilton or De Lancey? How does Hamilton respond to Bradley's citation of precedent?*

MR. CHIEF JUSTICE. Mr. Attorney, you have heard what Mr. *Hamilton* has said, and the Cases he has cited, for having his Witnesses examined, to prove the Truth of the several Facts contained in the Papers set forth in the Information, what do you say to it?

MR. ATTORNEY. The Law in my Opinion is very clear; they cannot be admitted to justify a Libel; for, by the Authorities I have already read to the Court, it is not the less a Libel because it is true. I think I need not trouble the Court with reading the Cases over again; the Thing seems to be very plain, and I submit it to the Court.

MR. CHIEF JUSTICE. Mr. *Hamilton*, the Court is of Opinion, you ought not to be permitted to prove the Facts in the Papers: These are the Words of the Book, *"It is far from being a Justification of a Libel, that the Contents thereof are true, or that the Person upon whom it is made, had a bad Reputation, since the greater Appearance there is of Truth in any malicious Invective, so much the more provoking it is."*[51]

MR. HAMILTON. These are Star Chamber Cases, and I was in hopes, that Practice had been dead with the Court.[52]

MR. CHIEF JUSTICE. Mr. *Hamilton*, the Court have delivered their Opinion, and we expect you will use us with good Manners; you are not to be permitted to argue against the Opinion of the Court.

MR. HAMILTON. With Submission, I have seen the Practice in very great Courts, and never heard it deemed unmannerly to———.

MR. CHIEF JUSTICE. After the Court have declared their Opinion, it is not good Manners to insist upon a Point, in which you are over-ruled.

MR. HAMILTON. I will say no more at this Time; the Court I see is against us in this Point; and that I hope I may be allowed to say.

MR. CHIEF JUSTICE. Use the Court with good Manners, and you shall be allowed all the Liberty you can reasonably desire.[53]

MR. HAMILTON. I thank Your Honour. Then Gentlemen of the Jury, it is to you we must appeal, for Witnesses to the Truth of the Facts we have offered, and are denied the Liberty to prove; and let it not seem strange, that I apply myself to you in this Manner, I am warranted so to do both by Law and Reason. The Law supposes you to be summoned, *out of the Neighbourhood where the Fact is alledged to be committed*; and the Reason of your being taken out of the Neighbourhood is, *because you are supposed to have the best Knowledge of the Fact that is to be tried*. And were you to find a Verdict against my Client, you must take upon you to say, the Papers referred to in the Information, and which we acknowledge we printed and published, are *false, scandalous and seditious*; but of this I can have no Apprehension. You are Citizens of *New-York*; you are really what the Law supposes you to be,

---

[51] The quotation is from Hawkins, *Pleas of the Crown*, 1:194, sec. 6.

[52] Hamilton's response here was risky. He essentially implied that Chief Justice De Lancey was acting as a tyrant, by pointing out to the jury and audience that De Lancey was relying on Star Chamber precedents.

[53] De Lancey's insistence that a lawyer cannot dispute the rulings of the court seems mostly a function of his youth and inexperience. Note that immediately after this exchange, Hamilton changes his argument by appealing directly to the jury to acquit in spite of the legal rulings against his client.

honest and lawful Men; and, according to my Brief, the Facts which we offer to prove were not committed in a Corner; they are notoriously known to be true; and therefore in your Justice lies our Safety. And as we are denied the Liberty of giving Evidence, to prove the Truth of what we have published, I will beg Leave to lay it down as a standing Rule in such Cases, *That the suppressing of Evidence ought always to be taken for the strongest Evidence*; and I hope it will have that Weight with you. But since we are not admitted to examine our Witnesses, I will endeavour to shorten the Dispute with Mr. Attorney, and to that End, I desire he would favour us with some Standard Definition of a Libel, by which it may be certainly known, whether a Writing be a Libel, yea or not.

MR. ATTORNEY. The Books, I think, have given a very full Definition of a Libel; they say it is *in a strict Sense taken for a malicious Defamation, expressed either in Printing or Writing, and tending either to blacken the Memory of one who is dead, or the Reputation of one who is alive, and to expose him to public Hatred, Contempt or Ridicule. §.2. But it is said, That in a larger Sense, the Notion of a Libel may be applied to any Defamation whatsoever, expressed either by Signs or Pictures, as by fixing up a Gallows against a Man's Door, or by painting him in a shameful and ignominious Manner. §.3. And since the chief Cause for which the Law so severely punishes all Offences of this Nature, is the direct Tendency of them to a Breach of Publick Peace, by provoking the Parties injured, their Friends and Families to Acts of Revenge, which it would be impossible to restrain by the severest Laws, were there no Redress from Publick Justice for Injuries of this kind, which of all others are most sensibly felt; and since the plain Meaning of such Scandal as is expressed by Signs or Pictures, is as obvious to common Sense, and as easily understood by every common Capacity, and altogether as provoking as that which is expressed by Writing or Printing, why should it not be equally criminal? § 4 And from the same Ground it seemeth also clearly to follow, That such scandal as is expressed in a scoffing and ironical Manner, makes a Writing as properly a Libel, as that which is expressed in direct Terms; as where a Writing, in a taunting Manner reckoning up several Acts of publick Charity done by one, says* You will not play the Jew, nor the Hypocrite, *and so goes on in a Strain of Ridicule to insinuate, that what he did was owing to his Vain-Glory; or where a Writing, pretending to recommend to one the Characters of several great Men for his Imitation, instead of taking Notice of what they are generally esteemed famous for, pitched on such Qualities only which their Enemies charge them with the Want of, as by proposing such a one to be imitated for his Courage, who is known to be a great Statesman, but no Soldier, and another to be imitated for his Learning, who is known to be a great General, but no Scholar, &c. which Kind of Writing is as well understood to mean only to upbraid the Parties with the Want of these Qualities, as if it had directly and expressly done so.*[54]

MR. HAMILTON. Ay, Mr. Attorney; but what Standard Rule have the Books laid down, by which we can certainly know, whether the Words or the Signs are malicious? Whether they are defamatory? Whether they tend to the Breach of the Peace, and a sufficient Ground to provoke a Man, his Family, or Friends to Acts of Revenge, especially those of the ironical sort of Words? And what Rule have you to know when I write ironically? I think it would be hard, when I say, *such a Man is a very worthy honest Gentleman, and of fine Understanding,* that therefore I meant *he was a Knave or a Fool.*

MR. ATTORNEY. I think the Books are very full; it is said in *I Hawk. p. 193,* just now read, *That such Scandal as is expressed in a scoffing and ironical Manner, makes a Writing as properly a Libel, as that which is expressed in direct Terms; as where a Writing, in a taunting Manner says, reckoning up several Acts of Charity done by one, says,* you will not play the Jew or the Hypocrite, *and so goes on to insinuate, that what he did was owing to his Vain-Glory, &c. Which Kind of Writing is as well understood to mean only to upbraid the Parties with the Want of these Qualities, as if it had directly and expressly done so.* I think nothing can be plainer or more full than these Words.

MR. HAMILTON. I agree the Words are very plain, and I shall not scruple to allow (when we are agreed that the Words are *false and scandalous, and were spoken in an ironical and scoffing Manner, &c.*) that they are really *libellous;* but here still occurs the Uncertainty, which makes the Difficulty to know, what Words are *scandalous,* and what not; for you say, they may be *scandalous, true* or *false;* besides, how shall we know whether the Words were spoke in a *scoffing and ironical Manner,* or seriously? Or how can you know, whether the Man did not think as he wrote? For by your Rule, if he did, it is no *Irony,* and consequently no *Libel.* But under Favour, Mr. Attorney, I think the same Book, and the same Section will shew us the only Rule by which all these Things are to be known. The Words are these; *which Kind of Writing is as well* UNDERSTOOD *to mean only to upbraid the Parties with the Want of these Qualities, as if they had directly and expressly done so.*[55] Here it

---

[54] *I Hawk. Chap.* LXXIII. § I. *& seq.* [Zenger]

[55] Hamilton is quoting from Hawkins, *Pleas of the Crown,* 1:193, just as the attorney general quoted from the same source on the two preceding pages of the *Brief Narrative.*

is plain, the Words are *scandalous, scoffing and ironical,* only as they are UNDERSTOOD. I know no Rule laid down in the Books but this, I mean, as the Words are *understood.*

MR. CHIEF JUSTICE. Mr. *Hamilton,* do you think it so hard to know, when Words are ironical, or spoke in a scoffing Manner?

MR. HAMILTON. I own it may be known; but I insist, the only Rule to know is, as I do or can *understand* them; I have no other Rule to go by, but as I *understand* them.

MR. CHIEF JUSTICE. That is certain. All Words are libellous or not, as they are *understood.* Those who are to judge of the Words, must judge whether they *are scandalous* or *ironical, tend to the Breach of the Peace,* or are *seditious:* There can be no Doubt of it.

MR. HAMILTON. I thank Your Honour; I am glad to find the Court of this Opinion. Then it follows that those twelve Men must *understand* the Words in the Information to be *scandalous,* that is to say *false;* for I think it is not pretended they are of the *ironical* Sort; and when they understand the Words to be so, they will say we are guilty of Publishing a *false Libel,* and not otherwise.

MR. CHIEF JUSTICE. No, Mr. *Hamilton;* the Jury may find that *Zenger* printed and published those Papers, and leave it to the Court to judge whether they are libellous; you know this is very common; it is in the Nature of a special Verdict,[56] where the Jury leave the Matter of Law to the Court.

MR. HAMILTON. I know, may it please Your Honour, the Jury may do so; but I do likewise know, they may do otherwise. I know they have the Right beyond all Dispute, to determine both the Law and the Fact, and where they do not doubt of the Law, they ought to do so. This of leaving it to [the] Judgment of the Court, *whether the Words are libellous or not,* in Effect renders Juries useless (to say no worse) in many Cases; but this I shall have Occasion to speak to by and by; and I will with the Court's Leave proceed to examine the Inconveniences that must inevitably arise from the Doctrines Mr. Attorney has laid down; and I observe, in support of this Prosecution, he has frequently repeated the Words taken from the Case of *Libel. famosus,* in *5 Co.*[57] This is indeed the leading Case, and to which almost all

[56] In a special verdict, the jury determines the relevant facts in the case (in this sense, the jury is the "finder of the facts"), but the jury leaves it to the judge to determine the proper application of the law to those facts.

[57] *The Case of Libellis Famosis,* 5 Coke's Reports 125 (1606). In this case, the Star Chamber set out the rules for determining what was seditious or criminal libel. Although Parliament had abolished the hated Star Chamber in 1641, the precedent of *Libellis Famosis* was still "good law" in England at the time of the Zenger case.

the other Cases upon the Subject of Libels do refer; and I must insist upon saying, That according as this Case seems to be understood by the [Court] and Mr. Attorney, it is not Law at this Day: For tho' I own it to be base and unworthy, to scandalize any Man, yet I think it is even vilainous to scandalize a Person of publick Character, and I will go so far into Mr. Attorney's Doctrine as to agree, that if the Faults, Mistakes, nay even the Vices of such a Person be private and personal, and don't affect the Peace of the Publick, or the Liberty or Property, of our Neighbour, it is unmanly and unmannerly to expose them either by Word or Writing. But when a Ruler of a People brings his personal Failings, but much more his Vices, into his Administration, and the People find themselves affected by them, either in their Liberties or Properties, that will alter the Case mightily; and all the high Things that are said in Favour of Rulers, and of Dignities, and upon the side of Power, will not be able to stop People's Mouths when they feel themselves oppressed, I mean in a free Government. It is true in Times past it was a Crime to speak Truth, and in that terrible Court of Star Chamber, many worthy and brave Men suffered for so doing; and yet even in that Court, and in those bad Times, a great and good Man durst say, what I hope will not be taken amiss of me to say in this Place, *to wit, The Practice of Informations for Libels is a Sword in the Hands of a wicked King, and an arrand Coward, to cut down and destroy the innocent; the one cannot, because of his high Station, and the other dares not, because of his Want of Courage, revenge himself in another Manner.*[58]

MR. ATTORNEY. Pray Mr. *Hamilton,* have a Care what you say, don't go too far neither, I don't like those Liberties.[59]

MR. HAMILTON. Sure, Mr. Attorney, you won't make any Applications; all Men agree that we are governed by the best of Kings, and I cannot see the Meaning of Mr. Attorney's Caution; my well known Principles, and the Sense I have of the Blessings we enjoy under His present Majesty, makes it impossible for me to err, and I hope, even to be suspected, in that Point of Duty to my King. May it please Your Honour, I was saying, that notwithstanding all the Duty and reverence

---

[58]Stanley N. Katz suggests that this obscure quotation is from the 1637 trial of John Lilburne. Katz, *Brief Narrative,* p. 228. Lilburne was tried under a Star Chamber decree, and thus the quotation reinforces the association between the prosecution and tyranny. See generally Pauline Gregg, *Free-Born John: A Biography of John Lilburne* (London: Harrap, 1961).

[59]Once again Hamilton implies that the prosecution of Zenger is like a Star Chamber case. This time he angers the attorney general, Bradley.

claimed by Mr. Attorney to Men in Authority, they are not exempt from observing the Rules of common Justice, either in their private or publick Capacities; the Laws of our Mother Country know no Exemption. It is true, Men in Power are harder to be come at for wrongs they do, either to a private Person, or to the publick; especially a Governour in the Plantations, where they insist upon an Exemption from Answering Complaints of any kind in their own Government. We are indeed told, and it is true they are obliged to answer a Suit in the King's Courts at *Westminster*, for a Wrong done to any Person here: But do we not know how impracticable this is to most Men among us, to leave their Families (who depend upon their Labour and Care for their Livelihood) and carry Evidences to *Britain*, and at a great, nay, a far greater Expense than almost any of us are able to bear, only to prosecute a Governour for an Injury done here. But when the Oppression is general there is no Remedy even that Way, no, our Constitution has (blessed be God) given Us an Opportunity, if not to have such Wrongs redressed, yet by our Prudence and Resolution we may in a great measure prevent the committing of such Wrongs, by making a Governour sensible that it is his interest to be just to those under his Care; for such is the Sense that Men in General (I mean Freemen) have of common Justice, that when they come to know, that a chief Magistrate abuses the Power with which he is trusted, for the good of the People, and is attempting to turn that very Power against the Innocent, whether of high or low degree, I say, Mankind in general seldom fail to interpose, and as far as they can, prevent the Destruction of their fellow Subjects. And has it not often been seen (I hope it will always be seen) that when the Representatives of a free People are by just Representations or Remonstrances, made sensible of the sufferings of their Fellow-Subjects, by the Abuse of Power in the Hands of a Governour, they have declared (and loudly too) that they were not obliged by any Law to support a Governour who goes about to destroy a Province or Colony, or their Privileges, which by His Majesty he was appointed, and by the Law he is bound to protect and encourage. But I pray it may be considered, of what Use is this mighty Privilege, if every Man that suffers must be silent? And if a Man must be taken up as a Libeller, for telling his sufferings to his Neighbour? I know it may be answered, *Have you not a Legislature? Have you not a House of Representatives to whom you may complain?* And to this I answer, we have. But what then? Is an Assembly to be troubled with every Injury done by a Governour? Or are they to hear of nothing but what those in the

Administration will please to tell them? Or what Sort of a Tryal must a Man have? And how is he to be remedied; especially if the Case were, as I have known it to happen in *America* in my Time; That a Governour who has Places (I will not [say] Pensions, for I believe they seldom give that to another which they can take to themselves) to bestow, and can or will keep the same Assembly (after he has modeled them so as to get a Majority of the House in his Interest) for near *twice Seven Years* together? I pray, what Redress is to be expected for a honest Man, who makes his Complaint against a Governour, to an Assembly who may properly enough be said, to be made by the same Governour against whom the Complaint is made? The Thing answers it self. No, it is natural, it is a Privilege, I will go farther, it is a Right which all Freemen claim, and are entitled to complain when they are hurt; they have a Right publickly to remonstrate the Abuses of Power, in the strongest Terms, to put their Neighbours upon their Guard, against the Craft or open Violence of Men in Authority, and to assert with Courage the Sense they have of the Blessings of Liberty, the Value they put upon it, and their Resolution at all Hazards to preserve it, as one of the greatest Blessings Heaven can bestow. And when a House of Assembly composed of honest Freemen sees the general Bent of the Peoples Inclinations, That is it which must and will (I'm sure it ought to) weigh with a Legislature, in Spite of all the Craft, Carressing and Cajoling, made use of by a Governour, to divert them from harkning to the Voice of their Country. And we all very well understand the true Reason, why Gentlemen take so much Pains and make such great Interest to be appointed Governours, so is the Design of their Appointment not less manifest. We know His Majesty's gracious Intentions to his Subjects; he desires no more than that his People in the Plantations should be kept up to their Duty and Allegiance to the Crown of *Great Britain*, that Peace may be preserved amongst them, and Justice impartially administred; that we may be governed so as to render us useful to our Mother Country, by encouraging us to make and raise such Commodities as may be useful to *Great Britain*. But will any one say, that all or any of these good Ends are to be effected, by a Governour's setting his People together by the Ears,[60] and by the Assistance of one Part of the People to plague and plunder the other? The Commission which Governour's bear, while they execute the Powers given them, according to the Intent of the Royal Grantor, expressed in their Commissions, requires

---

[60]Sowing dissension among the people.

and deserves very great Reverence and Submission; but when a Governour departs from the Duty enjoyned him by his Sovereign, and acts as if he was less accountable than the Royal Hand that gave him all that Power and Honour that he is possessed of; this sets People upon examining and enquiring into the Power, Authority, and Duty of such a Magistrate, and to compare those with his Conduct, and just as far as they find he exceeds the Bounds of his Authority, or falls short in doing impartial Justice to the People under his Administration, so far they very often, in return, come short in their Duty to such a Governour. For Power alone will not make a Man beloved, and I have heard it observed, That the Man who was neither good nor wise before his being made a Governour, never mended upon his Preferment, but has been generally observed to be worse: For Men who are not endued with Wisdom and Virtue, can only be kept in Bounds by the Law; and by how much the further they think themselves out of the Reach of the Law, by so much the more wicked and cruel Men are. I wish there were no Instances of the Kind at this Day. And wherever this happens to be the Case of a Governour, unhappy are the People under his Administration, and in the End he will find himself so too; for the People will neither love him nor support him. I make no Doubt but there are those here, who are zealously concerned for the Success of this Prosecution, and yet I hope they are not many, and even some of those, I am persuaded (when they consider to what Lengths such Prosecutions may be carried, and how deeply the Liberties of the People may be affected by such Means) will not all abide by their present Sentiments; I say, *Not All*: For the Man who from an Intimacy and Acquaintance with a Governour has conceived a personal Regard for him, the Man who has felt none of the Strokes of his Power, the Man who believes that a Governour has a Regard for him and confides in him, it is natural for such Men to wish well to the Affairs of such a Governour; and as they may be Men of Honour and Generosity, may, and no Doubt will, wish him Success, so far as the Rights and Privileges of their Fellow Citizens are not affected. But as Men of Honour, I can apprehend nothing from them; they will never exceed that Point. There are others that are under stronger Obligations, and those are such, as are in some Sort engaged in Support of a Governour's Cause, by their own or their Relations Dependance on his Favour, for some Post or Preferment; such Men have what is commonly called Duty and Gratitude, to influence their Inclinations, and oblige them to go his Lengths. I know Men's Interests are very near to them, and they will do much rather than foregoe the Favour of a Governour, and a Livelihood at the same Time; but I can with very just Grounds hope, even from those Men, whom I will suppose to be Men of Honour and Conscience too, that when they see, the Liberty of their Country is in Danger, either by their Concurrence, or even by their Silence, they will like *Englishmen*, and like themselves, freely make a Sacrifice of any Preferment or Favour rather than be accessary to destroying the Liberties of their Country, and entailing Slavery upon their Posterity. There are indeed another set of Men, of whom I have no Hopes, I mean such, who lay aside all other Considerations, and are ready to joyn with Power in any Shapes, and with any Man or Sort of Men, by whose Means or Interest they may be assisted to gratify their Malice and Envy against those whom they have been pleased to hate; and that for no other Reason, but because they are Men of Abilities and Integrity, or at least are possessed of some valuable Qualities, far superior to their own. But as Envy is the Sin of the Devil, and therefore very hard, if at all, to be repented of, I will believe there are but few of this detestable and worthless Sort of Men, nor will their Opinions or Inclinations have any influence upon this Tryal. But to proceed; I beg Leave to insist, That the Right of complaining or remonstrating is natural; And the Restraint upon this natural Right is the Law only, and that those Restraints can only extend to what is *false*: For as it is Truth alone which can excuse or justify any Man for complaining of a bad Administration, I as frankly agree, that nothing ought to excuse a Man who raises a false Charge or Accusation, even against a private Person, and that no manner of Allowance ought to be made to him, who does so against a publick Magistrate. *Truth* ought to govern the whole Affair of Libels, and yet the Party accused runs Risque enough even then; for if he fails in proving every Tittle of what he has wrote, and to the Satisfaction of the Court and Jury too, he may find to his Cost, that when the Prosecution is set on Foot by Men in Power, it seldom wants Friends to Favour it. And from thence (it is said) has arisen the great Diversity of Opinions among Judges about what Words were or were not scandalous or libellous. I believe it will be granted, that there is not greater Uncertainty in any Part of the Law, than about Words of Scandal; it would be mispending of the Court's Time to mention the Cases; they may be said to be numberless; and therefore the utmost Care ought to be taken in following Precedents; and the Times when the Judgments were given, which are quoted for Authorities in the Case of Libels, are much to be regarded. I think it will be agreed, That ever since the Time of the Star Chamber, where the most arbitrary and destructive Judgments and Opinions were given, that ever an *Englishman* heard of, at least in his own Country: I say, Prosecutions for Libels since the Time of that arbitrary Court, and until the glorious Revolution, have generally been set on Foot at the Instance of the Crown or its Ministers; and it is no small Reproach to the Law, that these Prosecutions were too often and too much countenanced by the Judges, who held their Places at Pleasure, (a disagreeable Tenure to any Officer, but a dangerous one in the Case of a Judge.) To say more to this Point may not be proper. And yet I cannot think it unwarrantable, to shew the unhappy influence that a Sovereign has sometimes had, not only upon Judges, but even upon Parliaments themselves.

Hamilton's Use of Precedent

In the following portion of the Narrative, *Hamilton invokes the weight and history of precedent in attempting to discredit the use of informations against British citizens and to convince the jurors that they can and must find Zenger not guilty of libel if they believe that his words contained "no falshood nor Sedition." Are Hamilton's precedents really useful to his case? Should old cases (precedent) govern the new realities of the American colonies?*

It has already been shewn, how the Judges differed in their Opinions about the Nature of a Libel, in the Case of the seven Bishops.[61] There you see three Judges of one Opinion, that is, of a wrong Opinion, in the Judgment of the best Men in *England*, and one Judge of a right Opinion. How unhappy might it have been for all of us at this Day, if that Jury had understood the Words in that Information as the Court did? Or if they had left it to the Court, to judge whether the Petition of the Bishops was or was not a Libel? No they took upon them, to their immortal Honour! To determine both *Law* and *Fact*, and to *understand* the Petition of the Bishops *to be no Libel, that is, to contain no falshood nor Sedition*, and therefore found them *Not Guilty*. And remarkable is the Case of Sir *Samuel Barnardiston*, who was fined 10,000£ for Writing a Letter, in which, it may be said, none saw any Scandal or Falshood but the Court and Jury; for that Judgment was afterwards looked upon as a cruel and detestable

[61] See note 19.

Judgment, and therefore was reversed by Parliament.[62] Many more Instances might be given of the Complaisance of Court-Judges, about those Times, and before; but I will mention only one Case more, and that is the Case of Sir *Edward Hales*,[63] who tho' a *Roman Catholick*, was by King *James* II, prefered to be a Colonel of his Army, notwithstanding the Statute of *Cha. 2d Chap.* 2,[64] by which it is provided, *That every one that accepts of an Office, Civil or Military, &c. shall take the Oaths, subscribe the Declaration, and take the Sacrament, within three Months, &c. otherwise he is disabled to hold such Office and the Grant for the same to be null and void, and the Party to forfeit 500£.* Sir *Edward Hales* did not take the Oaths or Sacrament, and was prosecuted for the 500£ for exercising the Office of a Colonel by the Space of three Months, without conforming as in the Act is directed. Sir *Edward* pleads, *That the King by His Letters Patents did dispence with his taking the Oaths and Sacrament, and subscribing the Declaration, and had pardoned the forfeiture of 500£.* And *whether the King's Dispensation was good, against the said Act of Parliament?* was the question. I shall mention no more of this Case, than to shew how in the Reign of an arbitrary Prince, where Judges hold their Seats at Pleasure, their Determinations have not always been such as to make Precedents of, but the Contrary; and so it happened in this Case, where it was solemnly judged, *That, notwithstanding this Act of Parliament, made in the strongest Terms, for Preservation of the Protestant Religion, That yet the King had, by His Royal Prerogative, a Power to dispence with that Law;* and Sir *Edward Hales* was acquitted by the Judges accordingly. So the King's Dispensing Power, being by the Judges set up above the Act of Parliament, this Law, which the People looked upon as their chief Security against Popery and Arbitrary Power, was by this Judgment rendered altogether ineffectual.[65] But this Judgment is sufficiently exposed by Sir *Edward Atkins*, late one of the Judges

[62] Hamilton is wrong here. Parliament did not reverse this fine. Katz, *Brief Narrative*, 237 n. 10.

[63] *Trial of Sir Edward Hales Bart. For Neglecting to Take the Oaths of Supremacy and Allegiance*, Court of Kings Bench, 11 Howell's State Trials 1165 (1686). The king appointed Hales to his position and then prosecuted him for not taking the oath. This was a collusive prosecution designed to get the court to affirm the king's power to appoint people who had not taken the oaths of supremacy and allegiance.

[64] The citation is to "An Act for preventing Dangers which may happen from Popish Recusants," 25 Ch. II, Cap. 2 (1673). This cite is to the twenty-fifth year of the reign of King Charles II. This was in fact a legal fiction. Charles actually reigned from 1660 to 1685. However, for legal purposes the years of his reign were measured from the execution of his father, King Charles I, January 30, 1649.

[65] King James II had tried, by royal fiat, to appoint Roman Catholics to some offices, in violation of laws prohibiting Catholics from holding those offices. The issue between the king and Parliament was not over religious toleration but over the power of the

of the Court of Common Pleas in his *Enquiry into the King's Power of dispensing with pœnal Statutes*;[66] where it is shewn, *Who it was that first invented Dispensations; how they came into* England; *what ill Use has been made of them there; and all this principally owing to the Countenance given them by the Judges.* He says of the Dispensing Power,[67] *The Pope was the Inventor of it; our Kings have borrowed it from them; and the Judges have from Time to Time nursed and dressed it up, and given it Countenance; and it is still upon the Growth, and encroaching, 'till it has almost subverted all Law, and made the regal Power absolute if not dissolute.* This seems not only to shew how far Judges have been influenced by Power, and how little Cases of this Sort, where the Prerogative has been in Question in former Reigns, are to be relied upon for Law: But I think it plainly shews too, that a Man may use a greater Freedom with the Power of His Sovereign and the Judges in *Great-Britain*, than it seems he may with the Power of a Governour in the Plantations, who is but a Fellow Subject. Are these Words with which we are charged, like these? Do Mr. *Zenger's* Papers contain any such Freedoms with his Governour or His Council, as Sir *Edward Atkins* has taken, with the Regal Power and the Judges in *England?* And yet I never heard of any Information brought against him for these Freedoms.

If then upon the whole there is so great an Uncertainty among Judges (learned and great Men) in Matters of this Kind; If Power has had so great an Influence on Judges; how cautious ought we to be in determining by their Judgments, especially in the Plantations, and in the Case of Libels? There is Heresy in Law, as well as in Religion, and both have changed very much; and we well know that it is not two Centuries ago that a Man would have been burnt as an Heretick, for owning such Opinions in Matters of Religion as are publickly wrote and printed at this Day. They were fallible Men, it seems, and we take the Liberty not only to differ from them in religious Opinions, but to condemn them and their Opinions too; and I must presume, that in taking these Freedoms in thinking and speaking about Matters of Faith or Religion, we are in the right: For tho' it is said there are very great Liberties of this Kind taken in *Newe York*, yet I have heard of no Information preferred by Mr. Attorney for any Offences of this Sort. From which I think it is pretty clear, That in *New-York*, a Man may make very free with his God, but he must take special Care what he says of his Governour. It is agreed upon

---

king to overrule acts of Parliament. This dispute led to the Glorious Revolution and the overthrow of King James II.

[66]Sir *Edw. Atkins's* Enquiry into the Power of Dispensing with pœnal Statutes. [Zenger]

[67]Postscript to the *Enquiry pag.* 51. [Zenger]

by all Men, that this is a Reign of Liberty; and while Men keep within the Bounds of Truth, I hope they may with Safety both speak and write their Sentiments of the Conduct of Men in Power I me[a]n of that Part of their Conduct only, which affects the Liberty or Property of the People under their Administration; were this to be denied, then the next Step may make them Slaves: For what Notions can be entertained of Slavery, beyond that of suffering the greatest injuries and Oppressions, without the Liberty of complaining; or if they do, to be destroyed, Body and Estate, for so doing?

It is said and insisted on by Mr. Attorney, *That Government is a sacred Thing; That it is to be supported and reverenced; It is Government that protects our Persons and Estates; That prevents Treasons, Murders, Robberies, Riots, and all the Train of Evils that overturns Kingdoms and States, and ruins particular Persons; and if those in the Administration, especially the Supream Magistrate must have all their Conduct censured by private Men, Government cannot subsist.* This is called a *Licentiousness not to be tollerated.* It is said, *That it brings the Rulers of the People into Contempt, and their Authority not to be regarded, and so in the End the Laws cannot be put in Execution.* These I say, and such as these, are the general Topicks insisted upon by Men in Power, and their Advocates. But I wish it might be considered at the same Time, How often it has happened, that the Abuse of Power has been the primary Cause of these Evils, and that it was the Injustice and Oppression of these great Men, which has commonly brought them into Contempt with the People. The Craft and Art of such Men is great, and who, that is the least acquainted with History or Law, can be ignorant of the specious Pretenses, which have often been made use of by Men in Power, to introduce arbitrary Rule, and destroy the Liberties of a free People. I will give two Instances; and as they are Authorities not to be denied, nor can be misunderstood, I presume they will be sufficient.

The *first* is the Statute of *3d* of *Hen. 7. Cap. I.* The Preamble of the Statute will prove all, and more than I have alledged. It begins, *"The King Our Sovereign Lord remembereth how by unlawful Maintenances, giving of Liveries, Signs and Tokens, &c. untrue Demeanings of Sheriffs in making of Pannels, and other untrue Returns, by taking of Money, by Injuries, by great Riots and unlawful Assemblies; the Policy and good Rule of this Realm is almost subdued; and for the not punishing these Inconveniences, and by Occasion of the Premisses, little or nothing may be found by Inquiry, &c. to the increase of Murders, &c. and unsureties of all Men living, and Losses of their Lands and Goods."* Here is a fine and specious Pretense for introducing the Remedy, as it is called, which is provided by this Act, *that is*; instead of being lawfully accused by 24 good and lawful Men of the Neighbourhood, and afterwards tried by 12 like lawful Men,[68] here is a Power given to the Lord Chancellor, Lord Treasurer, the Keeper of the King's privy Seal, or two of them, calling to them a Bishop, a temporal Lord, and other great Men mentioned in the Act, (whom, it is to be observed, were all to be Dependants on the Court) to receive Information against any Person for any of the Misbehaviours recited in that Act, and by their Discretion to examine, and to punish them according to their demerit.

The second Statute I proposed to mention, is the *11th* of the same King, *Chap. 3d*, the Preamble of which Act has the like fair Pretenses as the former; *for the King calling to his Remembrance the good Laws made against the receiving of Liveries, &c. unlawful Extortions, Maintenances, Embracery, &c. unlawful Games, &c. and many other great Enormitys, and Offences committed against many good Statutes, to the Displeasure of Almighty God, which*, the Act says, *could not, nor yet can, be conveniently punished by the due Order of the Law, except it were first found by 12 Men, &c. which, for the Causes aforesaid, will not find nor yet present the Truth.* And therefore the same Statute directs, *that the Justices of Assize, and Justices of the Peace, shall, upon Information for the King before them made, have full Power, by their Discretion, to hear and determine all such Offences.* Here are two Statutes that are allowed to have given the deepest Wound to the Liberties of the People of *England* of any that I remember to have been made, unless it may be said, that the Statute made in the Time of *Henry 8th*, by which his Proclamations were to have the effect of Laws, might in its Consequence be worse.[69] And yet we see the plausible Pretenses found out by the great Men to procure these Acts. And it may justly be said, That by those Pretenses the People of *England* were cheated or aw'd into the Delivering up their antient and sacred Rights of Tryals by Grand and the Petit Juries. I hope to be excused for this Expression, seeing my Lord *Coke* calls it *an unjust and strange Act, that tended in its execution to the great Displeasure of Almighty God, and the utter subversion of the common Law.*[70]

These, I think, make out what I alledged, and are flagrant Instances of the Influence of Men in Power, even upon the Representatives of a whole Kingdom. From all which I hope it will be agreed, that it is a Duty which all good Men owe to their Country, to guard against the unhappy

[68]The reference is to the grand jury, of twenty-four citizens, and the petit or trial jury, of twelve.
[69]31 Henry VIII, chapter 8.
[70]4 *Inst.* [Zenger]

ill Men when intrusted with Power; and especially against
res and Dependants, who, as they are generally more neces-
urely more covetous and cruel. But it is worthy of Observation, that tho' the Spirit of Liberty was borne down and oppressed in
England at that Time, yet it was not lost; for the Parliament laid hold
of the first Opportunity to free the Subject from the many insufferable
Oppressions and Outrages committed upon their Persons and Estates
by Colour of these Acts, the last of which being deemed the most grievous, was repealed in the first Year of *Hen. 8th.*[71] Tho' it is to be observed,
that *Hen. 7th* and his Creatures reap'd such great Advantages by the
grievous Oppressions and Exactions, *grinding the Faces of the poor Subjects*, as my Lord *Coke* says, by Colour of this Statute by information
only, that a Repeal of this Act could never be obtained during the Life
of that Prince. The other Statute being the favourite Law for Supporting
arbitrary Power, was continued much longer. The Execution of it was
by the great Men of the Realm; and how they executed it, the Sense
of the Kingdom, expressed in the *17th* of *Charles 1st.* (by which the
Court of Star-chamber, the soil where Informations grew rankest) will
best declare.[72] In that Statute *Magna Charta*, and the other Statutes
made in the Time of *Edw. 3d.* which, I think, are no less than five, are
particularly enumerated as Acts, by which the Liberties and Privileges
of the People of *England* were secured to them, against such oppressive
Courts as the Star Chamber and others of the like Jurisdiction. And the
Reason assigned for their pulling down the Star Chamber, is *That the
Proceedings, Censures and Decrees of the Court of Star Chamber, even tho'
the great Men of the Realm, nay and a Bishop too* (holy Man) *were Judges,
had by Experience been found to be an intolerable Burthen to the Subject,
and the Means to introduce an arbitrary Power and Government.* And
therefore the Court was taken away, with all the other Courts in that
Statute mentioned, having like Jurisdiction.

I don't mention this Statute, as if by the taking away the Court of Star
Chamber, the Remedy for many of the Abuses or Offences censured
there, was likewise taken away; no, I only intend by it to shew, that the
People of *England* saw clearly the Danger of trusting their Liberties
and Properties to be tried, even by the greatest Men in the Kingdom,

---

[71] 1 Henry VIII, chapter 6.

[72] According to Katz, "Hamilton must have intended to refer to 16 Car. [Charles] I c.
10, the act which abolished the Court of Star Chamber, expounding the evils of arbitrary
justice. The parenthetical phrase probably ought to read: 'by which the Court of Star
Chamber, the soil where informations grew rankest, *was abolished.*'" Katz, *Brief Narrative*, 228 n. 47.

without the Judgment of a Jury of their Equals. They had felt the terrible effects of leaving it to the Judgment of these great Men to say what was *scandalous and seditious, false or ironical.* And if the Parliament of *England* thought this Power of judging was too great to be trusted with Men of the first Rank in the Kingdom, without the Aid of a Jury, how sacred soever their Characters might be, and therefore restored to the People their original Right of tryal by Juries, I hope to be excused for insisting, that by the Judgment of a Parliament, from whence an Appeal lies, the Jury are the proper Judges, of what is *false* at least, if not, of what is *scandalous and seditious.* This is an Authority not to be denied, it is as plain as it is great, and to say, that this Act indeed did restore to the People Tryals by Juries, which was not the Practice of the Star Chamber, but that did not give the Jurors any new Authority, or any Right to try Matters of Law, I say this Objection will not avail; for I must insist, that where Matter of Law is complicated with Matter of Fact, the Jury have a Right to determine both. As for Instance; upon Indictment for Murder, the Jury may, and almost constantly do, take upon them to Judge whether the Evidence will amount to Murder or Manslaughter, and find accordingly; and I must say I cannot see, why in our Case the Jury have not at least as good a Right to say, whether our News Papers are a Libel or no Libel as another Jury has to say, whether killing of a Man is Murder or Manslaughter. The Right of the Jury, to find such a Verdict as they in their Conscience do think is agreeable to their Evidence, is supported by the Authority of *Bushel's* Case, in *Vaughan's Reports, pag. 135,* beyond any Doubt.[73] For, in the Argument of that Case, the Chief Justice who delivered the Opinion of the Court, lays it down for Law, *That in all General Issues, as upon* Non Cul. *in* Trespass, Non Tort. Nul Disseizin *in* Assize, &c. *tho' it is Matter of Law, whether the Defendant is a Trespasser, a Disseizer, &c. in the particular Cases in Issue, yet the Jury find not (as*

[73] *Bushell's Case,* 6 Howell's State Trials 999 (1670), arose from the prosecution of the Quaker leader William Penn for his refusal to cease preaching in England. *The Trial of William Penn and William Mead, at Old Bailey, for a Tumultuous Assembly,* 6 Howell's State Trials 951 (1670). When the jury acquitted Penn, the Crown kept the jurors locked up for three days—without food—in order to persuade them to reach a guilty verdict. When this failed, the Crown fined and imprisoned Bushell and other jurors. In *Bushell's Case,* Chief Justice John Vaughan of the court of common pleas ruled that jurors could not be prosecuted for rendering a verdict, even if the Crown thought it was against the evidence. This case was a powerful precedent for the right of jurors, on their own, to acquit defendants charged with political crimes. Had Zenger pleaded innocent to the charge of actually printing the *Weekly Journal,* the jury in New York could have relied on the precedent in *Bushell's Case* to acquit him. Andrew Hamilton argued that *Bushell's Case* allowed the jury to render a general verdict of "not guilty" in a libel case, even though the defendant (Zenger) had admitted he published the offensive newspapers.

*in a special Verdict) the fact of every Case, leaving the Law to the Court;
but find for the Plaintiff or Defendant upon the Issue to be tried, wherein
they resolve both Law and Fact complicately.*[74] It appears by the same
Case, that tho' the discreet and lawful Assistance of the Judge, by Way
of Advice, to the Jury, may be useful; yet that Advice or Direction ought
always to be *upon Supposition, and not positive, and upon Coersion.*[75] The
Reason given in the same Book is *because the Judge (as Judge) cannot
know what the Evidence is which the Jury have,* that is, *he can only know
the Evidence given in Court: but the Evidence which the Jury have, may be
of their own Knowledge, as they are returned of the Neighbourhood.*[76] *They
may also know from their own Knowledge, that what is sworn in Court is
not true; and they may know the Witnesses to be stigmatized, to which the
Court may be strangers.*[77] But what is to my Purpose, is, that suppose
the Court did really know all the Evidence which the Jury know, yet in
that Case it is agreed, *That the Judge and Jury may differ in the Result of
their Evidence as well as two Judges may,* which often happens. And in
pag. 148, the Judge subjoins the Reason, why it is no Crime for a Jury
to differ in Opinion from the Court, where he says, *That a Man cannot
see with another's Eye, nor hear by another's Ear; no more can a Man conclude or infer the Thing by another's Understanding or Reasoning.* From
all which (I insist) it is very plain, *That the Jury are by Law at Liberty
(without any affront to the Judgment of the Court) to find both the Law and
the Fact, in our Case,* as they did in the case I am speaking to, which I
will beg Leave just to mention, and it was this. Mr. *Penn* and *Mead* being
Quakers, and having met in a peaceable Manner, after being shut out of
their Meeting House, preached in *Grace Church Street* in *London,* to the
People of their own Perswasion, and for this they were indicted; and it
was said, *That they with other Persons, to the Number of 300, unlawfully
and tumultuously assembled, to the Disturbance of the Peace, &c.* To which
they pleaded, *Not Guilty.* And the Petit Jury being sworn to try the issue
between the King and the Prisoners, that is, whether they were Guilty,
according to the Form of the Indictment? Here there was no Dispute but
they were assembled together, to the Number mentioned in the Indictment; But *whether that Meeting together was riotously, tumultuously, and
to the Disturbance of the Peace?* was the question. And the Court told the

[74] *Vaughan's Rep. p. 150.* [Zenger]
[75] *pag. 144.* [Zenger]
[76] *pag. 147.* [Zenger]
[77] At this time, courts presumed that jurors knew more facts about the case than
might be brought out at a trial and that they would use those facts to help decide the
case. This was based on the assumption that the jurors were members of the community
where the alleged crime took place.

Jury it was, and ordered the Jury to find it so; *For* (said the Court) *the Meeting was the Matter of Fact, and that is confessed, and we tell you it is unlawful, for it is against the Statute; and the Meeting being unlawful, it follows of Course that it was tumultuous, and to the Disturbance of the Peace.* But the Jury did not think fit to take the Court's Word for it, for they could neither find *Riot, Tumult,* or any Thing tending to the *Breach of the Peace* committed at that Meeting; and they acquitted Mr. *Penn* and *Mead.*[78] In doing of which they took upon them to judge both the *Law* and the *Fact,* at which the Court (being themselves true Courtiers) were so much offended, that they fined the Jury 40 Marks a piece, and committed them till paid. But Mr. *Bushel,* who valued the Right of a Juryman and the Liberty of his Country more than his own, refused to pay the Fine, and was resolved (tho' at great Expense and trouble too) to bring, and did bring, his *Habeas Corpus,* to be relieved from his Fine and Imprisonment, and he was released accordingly; and this being the Judgment in his Case, it is established for Law, *That the Judges, how great soever they be, have no Right to fine imprison or punish a Jury, for not finding a Verdict according to the Direction of the Court.*[79] And this I hope is sufficient to prove, That Jurymen are to see with their own Eyes, to hear with their own Ears, and to make use of their own Consciences and Understandings, in judging of the Lives, Liberties or Estates of their fellow Subjects. And so I have done with this Point.

This is the second information for Libelling of a Governour, that I have known in *America.* And the first, tho' it may look like a Romance, yet as it is true, I will beg Leave to mention it. Governour *Nicholson,* who happened to be offended with one [of] his Clergy, met him one Day upon the Road, and as was usual with him (under the Protection of his Commission) used the poor Parson with the worst of Language, threatened to cut off his Ears, slit his Nose, and at last to shoot him through the Head. The Parson being a reverend Man, continued all this Time uncovered in the Heat of the Sun, until he found an Opportunity to fly for it; and coming to a Neighbours House felt himself very ill of a Feaver, and immediately writes for a Doctor; and that his Physician might the better judge of his Distemper, he acquainted him with the Usage he had received; concluding, that the Governour was certainly mad, for that no Man in his Senses would have behaved in that manner. The Doctor unhappily shews the Parsons Letter; the Governour came to hear of it; and so an Information was prefered against the poor Man for saying *he*

---

[78] *The Trial of William Penn and William Mead, at Old Bailey, for a Tumultuous Assembly,* 6 Howell's State Trials 951 (1670).
[79] *Bushell's Case;* see note 73 for a discussion of this case.

believed the Governour was mad; and it was laid in the Information to be *false, scandalous* and *wicked, and wrote with Intent to move Sedition among the People, and bring His Excellency into Contempt.* But by an Order from the late Queen *Anne*, there was a Stop put to that Prosecution, with sundry others set on foot by the same Governour, against Gentlemen of the greatest Worth and Honour in that Government.[80]

And may not I be allowed, after all this, to say, That by a little Countenance, almost any Thing which a Man writes, may with the Help of that useful Term of Art, called an *Innuendo*, be construed to be a Libel, according to Mr. Attorney's Definition of it, That *whether the Words are spoke of a Person of a publick Character, or of a private Man, whether dead or Living, good or bad, true or false* all make a Libel; for according to Mr. Attorney, *after a Man hears a Writing read, or reads and repeats it, or laughs at it, they are all punishable.* It is true, Mr. Attorney is so good as to allow, *after the Party knows it to be a Libel*, but he is not so kind as to take the Man's Word for it.

Here were several Cases put to shew, That tho' what a Man writes of a Governour was true, proper and necessary, yet according to the foregoing Doctrine it might be construed to be a Libel: But Mr. Hamilton after the Tryal was over, being informed, That some of the Cases he had put, had really happened in this Government, he declared he had never heard of any such; and as he meant no personal Reflections he was sorry he had mentioned them, and therefore they are omitted here.

Concluding the Trial

The trial concludes with an accounting of Hamilton's final arguments, a summation of Bradley's closing remarks, and the chief justice's final charge to the jury, after which the jury deliberates and then returns its verdict. What rhetorical strategies does Hamilton employ in an effort to secure the sympathies of the jury for his client? What is the meaning of the

---

[80]This seems to refer to an encounter in 1704 between Francis Nicholson, who was the governor of Virginia, and Reverend John Munro. Nicholson encountered Munro on the road and apparently beat him. Munro complained to a number of people, and Nicholson had him prosecuted for "odious reflections" on the governor. Shortly after this, royal authorities recalled Nicholson. "Somehow after that recall an order from England ended the prosecution." Leonard W. Levy, *The Emergence of a Free Press* (New York: Oxford University Press, 1995), 20. While Hamilton's reference was to Nicholson as governor of Virginia, it also had special meaning to the New York jurors, because Nicholson had been lieutenant governor of New York for a brief time in 1688.

passage from an earlier case that De Lancey reads to the jury, and what impact did he hope it would have?

MR. HAMILTON. If a Libel is understood in the large and unlimited Sense urged by Mr. Attorney, there is scarce a Writing I know that may not be called a Libel, or scarce any Person safe from being called to an Account as a Libeller: For *Moses*, meek as he was, libelled *Cain*; and who is it that has not libelled the Devil? For according to Mr. Attorney it is no Justification to say one has a bad Name. *Echard* has libelled our good King *William: Burnet* has libelled among many others King *Charles* and King *James*; and *Rapin* has libelled them all.[81] How must a Man speak or write, or what must he hear, read or sing? Or when must he laugh, so as be secure from being taken up as a Libeller? I sincerely believe, that were some Persons to go thro' the Streets of *New-York* now-a-days, and read a Part of the Bible, if it was not known to be such, Mr. Attorney, with the help of his *Innuendo's*, would easily turn it into a Libel. As for instance, *Is. IX. 16, The Leaders of the People cause them to err, and they that are led by them are destroyed.*[82] But should Mr. Attorney go about to make this a Libel, he would read it thus; *The Leaders of the People* [*innuendo*, the Governour and Council of *New-York*] *cause them* [*innuendo*, the People of this Province] *to err, and they* [the People of this Province meaning] *that are led by them* [the Governour and Council meaning] *are destroyed* [*innuendo*, are deceived into the Loss of their Liberty] which is the worst Kind of Destruction. Or if some Persons should publickly repeat, in a Manner not pleasing to his Betters, the *10th* and *11th* Verses of the *LVI Chap.* of the same Book, there Mr. Attorney would have a large Field to display his Skill, in the artful Application of his *Innuendo's*. The Words are, *His Watchmen are all blind, they are ignorant, &c. Yea, they are greedy dogs, that can never have enough.* But to make them a Libel, there is according to Mr. Attorney's Doctrine, no more wanting but the Aid of his Skill, in the right adapting his *Innuendo's*, As for Instance; *His Watchmen* [*innuendo*, the Governour's Council and Assembly] *are* [all] *blind, they are ignorant* [*innuendo*, will not see

[81]The references are to Laurence Echard, *The History of England from the First Entrance of Julius Caesar to 1688* (London, 1707–1718); Laurence Echard, *The History of the Revolution and the Establishment of England in 1688* (London, 1725); Gilbert Burnet, *History of His Own Time*; and Paul de Raphin-Thoyras, *The History of England*, ed. Nichola Tindal (London, 1725–1731).

[82]*Isaiah* 9:16.

the dangerous Designs of His Excellency] *Yea, they* [the Governour and Council meaning] *are greedy Dogs, which can never have enough* [*innuendo*, enough of Riches and Power].[83] Such an Instance as this is seems only fit to be laugh'd at; but I may appeal to Mr. Attorney himself, whether these are not at least equally proper to be applied to His Excellency and His Ministers, as some of the Inferences and *Innuendo's* in his Information against my Client. Then if Mr. Attorney is at Liberty to come into Court, and file an Information in the King's Name, without Leave, who is secure, whom he is pleased to prosecute as a Libeller? And as the Crown Law is contended for in bad Times, there is no Remedy for the greatest Oppression of this Sort, even tho the Party prosecuted is acquitted with Honour. And give me Leave to say, as great Men as any in *Britain*, have boldly asserted, That the Mode of Prosecuting by Information (when a Grand Jury will not find *Billa vera*) is a national Grievance, and greatly inconsistent with that Freedom, which the Subjects of *England* enjoy in most other Cases.[84] But if we are so unhappy as not to be able to ward off this Stroke of Power directly, yet let us take Care not to be cheated out of our Liberties, by Forms and Appearances; let us always be sure that the Charge in the Information is made out clearly even beyond a Doubt; for tho Matters in the Information may be called *Form* upon Tryal, yet they may be, and often have been found to be *Matters of Substance* upon giving Judgment.

Gentlemen, The Danger is great, in Proportion to the Mischief that may happen, through our too great Credulity. A proper Confidence in a Court, is commendable; but as the Verdict (what ever it is) will be yours, you ought to refer no Part of your Duty to the Discretion of other Persons. If you should be of the Opinion, that there is no Falshood in Mr. *Zenger's* Papers, you will, nay (pardon me for the Expression) you ought to say so; because you don't know whether others (I mean the Court) may be of that Opinion. It is your Right to do so, and there is much depending upon your Resolution, as well as upon your Integrity.

The loss of liberty to a generous Mind, is worse than Death; and yet we know there have been those in all Ages, who for the sake of

---

[83] *Isaiah* 6:10–11.

[84] *Billa vera* means "true bill." The words "true bill" are "endorsed on a bill of indictment when a grand jury, after having heard the witnesses for the government, are of opinion there is sufficient cause to put the defendant on trial. Formerly, the endorsement was *Billa vera*, when legal proceedings were in Latin." John Bouvier, *A Law Dictionary Adapted to the Constitution and Laws of the United States of America* (Philadelphia: T. & J. W. Johnson, 1839), 2:455.

Preferment, or some imaginary Honour, have freely lent a helping Hand, to oppress, nay to destroy their Country. This brings to my Mind that saying of the immortal *Brutus*, when he look'd upon the Creatures of *Cæsar*, who were very great Men, but by no Means good Men. *"You* Romans," *said* Brutus, *"if yet I may call you so, consider what you are doing; remember that you are assisting Cæsar to forge those very Chains, which one day he will make your selves wear.*[85] This is what every Man (that values Freedom) ought to consider: He should act by Judgment and not by Affection or Self-Interest; for, where those prevail, No Ties of either Country or Kindred are regarded; as upon the other Hand, the Man, who loves his Country, prefers it's Liberty to all other Considerations, well knowing that without Liberty, Life is a Misery.

A famous Instance of this you will find in the History of another brave *Roman* of the same Name, I mean *Lucius Junius Brutus*, whose story is well known and therefore I shall mention no more of it, than only to shew the Value he put upon the Freedom of his Country. After this great Man, with his Fellow Citizens whom he had engag'd in the Cause, had banish'd *Tarquin* the Proud, the last King of *Rome*, from a Throne which he ascended by inhuman Murders and possess'd by the most dreadful Tyranny and Proscriptions, and had by this Means, amass'd incredible Riches, even sufficient to bribe to his Interest, many of the young Nobility of *Rome*, to assist him in recovering the crown; but the Plot being discovered, the principal Conspirators were apprehended, among whom were two of the Sons of *Junius Brutus.* It was absolutely necessary that some should be made Examples of, to deter others from attempting the restoring of *Tarquin* and destroying the Liberty of *Rome*. And to effect this it was, that *Lucius Junius Brutus*, one of the Consuls of *Rome*, in the Presence of the *Roman* People, sat Judge and condemned his own Sons, as Traitors to their Country: And to give the last Proof of his exalted Virtue, and his Love of Liberty: He with a Firmness of Mind, (only becoming so great a Man) caus'd their Heads to be struck off in his own Presence; and when he observ'd that his rigid Virtue, occasion'd a sort of Horror among the People, it is observ'd he only said. *"My Fellow-Citizens, do not think that this Proceeds from any Want of natural Affection: No, The Death of the Sons of* Brutus *can affect* Brutus *only; but the Loss of Liberty will affect my Country."*[86] Thus highly was Liberty esteem'd in those Days

[85]This quotation appears to be entirely made-up.
[86]Lucius Junius Brutus was one of the first two consuls of Rome, in about 509 BCE. For the story of how Brutus became counsel, see Livy [Titus Livus], *The History of*

110 BRIEF NARRATIVE OF THE TRYAL OF JOHN PETER ZENGER

that a Father could sacrifice his Sons to save his Country, But why do I go to Heathen *Rome*, to bring Instances of the Love of Liberty, the best Blood in *Britain* has been shed in the Cause of Liberty; and the Freedom we enjoy at this Day, may be said to be (in a great Measure) owing to the glorious Stand the famous *Hamden*, and other of our Countrymen, made against the arbitrary Demands, and illegal Impositions, of the Times in which they lived; who rather than give up the Rights of *Englishmen*, and submit to pay an illegal Tax, of no more, I think, than 3 shillings, resolv'd to undergo, and for their Liberty of their Country did undergo the greatest Extremities, in that arbitrary and terrible Court of Star Chamber, to whose arbitrary Proceedings, (it being compos'd of the principal Men of the Realm, and calculated to support arbitrary Government) no Bounds or Limits could be set, nor could any other Hand remove the Evil but a Parliament.[87]

Power may justly be compar'd to a great River, while kept within its due Bounds, is both Beautiful and Useful; but when it overflows, its Banks, it is then too impetuous to be stemm'd, it bears down all before it, and brings Destruction and Desolation wherever it comes. If then this is the Nature of Power, let us at least do our Duty, and like wise Men (who value Freedom) use our utmost Care to support Liberty, the only Bulwark against lawless Power, which in all Ages has sacrificed to it's wild Lust and boundless Ambition, the Blood of the best Men that ever liv'd.

I hope to be pardon'd Sir for my Zeal upon this Occasion; it is an old and wise Caution: *That when our Neighbour's House is on Fire, we ought to take Care of our own.*[88] For tho' Blessed be God, I live in

---

Rome, 1:56–60. For a discussion of the execution of his sons, see Livy, 2:5. Like the previous quotation, there seems to be no source for this quotation, and it was most likely made-up.

[87] Starting in 1629, King Charles I began to rule without Parliament. In 1636, without parliamentary authorization, the king attempted to collect a tax from all property owners in England to pay for ships necessary to defend the realm. Known as "Ship Money," such a tax had previously been levied only against people living in coastal areas. John Hampden, a minor Puritan leader, refused to pay the tax, but in a vote of seven to five the judges of the Court of Exchequer upheld the right of the king to tax his subjects without parliamentary authorization. This led to his prosecution in *Proceedings in the Case of Ship-Money, Between the King and John Hampden, Esq.,* 3 Howell's State Trials 826 (1637). Hampden became a symbol of resistance to arbitrary royal rule. See Esther S. Cope, *Politics without Parliament*, 1629–1640 (London: Allen & Unwin, 1987), 117–20. Significantly, Hampden lost his case in the Exchequer Court, which was the type of court Cosby tried to create to hear his suit against Van Dam.

[88] This is an English proverb, first published by John Rey, *English Proverbs* 105 (1678), from *Macmillan Book of Proverbs, Maxims, and Famous Phrases* (New York: Macmillan, 1976), 1675. However, the concept is Roman in origin, going back to Ovid, *Remediorum Amoris*, 1:625 (ca. 1 BCE).

a Government where Liberty is well understood, and freely enjoy'd: yet Experience has shewn us all (I'm sure it has to me) that a bad Precedent in one Government, is soon set up for an Authority in another; and therefore I cannot but think it mine, and every Honest Man's Duty, that (while we pay all due Obedience to Men in Authority) we ought at the same Time to be upon our Guard against Power, wherever we apprehend that it may affect ourselves or our Fellow-Subjects.

I am truly very unequal to such an Undertaking on many Accounts. And you see I labour under the Weight of many Years, and am born down with great Infirmities of Body; yet Old and Weak as I am,[89] I should think it my Duty if required, to go to the utmost Part of the Land, where my Service cou'd be of any Use in assisting to quench the Flame of Prosecutions upon Informations, sct on Foot by the Government, to deprive a People of the Right of Remonstrating, (and complaining too) of the arbitrary Attempts of Men in Power. Men who injure and oppress the People under their Administration provoke them to cry out and complain; and then make that very Complaint the Foundation for new Oppressions and Prosecutions. I wish I could say there were no Instances of this Kind. But to conclude; the Question before the Court and you Gentlemen of the Jury, is not of small nor private Concern, it is not the Cause of the poor Printer, nor of *New-York* alone, which you are now trying: No! It may in it's Consequence, affect every Freeman that lives under a British Government on the main of *America*. It is the best Cause. It is the Cause of Liberty; and I make no Doubt but your upright Conduct, this Day, will not only entitle you to the Love and Esteem of your Fellow-Citizens; but every Man who prefers Freedom to a Life of slavery will bless and honour You, as Men who have baffled the Attempt of Tyranny; and by an impartial and uncorrupt Verdict, have laid a noble Foundation for securing to ourselves, our Posterity, and our Neighbours, That, to which Nature and the Laws of our Country have given us a Right,—the Liberty—both of exposing and opposing arbitrary Power (in these Parts of the World, at least) by speaking and writing Truth.

Here Mr. Attorney observ'd, that Mr. Hamilton *had gone very much out of the Way, and had made himself and the People very merry: But that he*

---

[89]Hamilton was fifty-nine at the time but had some physical ailments that made him appear older. He may have been seeking the sympathy of the jury here by pointing to his age, but he might just as well have been contrasting his age and experience, and his willingness to fight corruption at such an age, with the youth, inexperience, and apparent corruption of the thirty-one-year-old Chief Justice De Lancey.

had been citing Cases, not at all to the Purpose; he said, there was no such Cause as Mr. Bushel's or Sir Edward Hales before the Court; and he could not find out what the Court or Jury had to do with Dispensations, Riots or unlawful Assemblies: All that the Jury had to consider of was Mr. Zenger's Printing and Publishing two scandalous Libels, which very highly reflected on his Excellency and the principal Men concern'd in the Administration of this Government, which is confess'd. That is, the Printing and Publishing of the Journals set forth in the Information is confess'd. And concluded that as Mr. Hamilton had confess'd the Printing, and there could be no doubt but they were scandalous Papers, highly reflecting upon his Excellency, and the principal Magistrates in the Province. And therefore he made no Doubt but the Jury would find the Defendant Guilty, and would refer to the Court for their Direction.

MR. CHIEF JUSTICE. Gentlemen of the Jury. The great Pains Mr. *Hamilton* has taken, to shew how little Regard Juries are to Pay to the Opinion of the Judges; and his insisting so much upon the Conduct of some Judges in Tryals of this kind; is done no doubt, with a Design that you should take but very little Notice, of what I might say upon this Occasion, I shall therefore only observe to you that, as the Facts or Words in the Information are confessed: The only Thing that can come in Question before you is, whether the Words as set forth in the Information make a Lybel. And that is a Matter of Law, no Doubt, and which you may leave to the Court. But I shall trouble you no further with any Thing more of my own, but read to you the Words of a learned and upright Judge[90] in a case of the like Nature.

To say that corrupt Officers are appointed to administer Affairs, is certainly a Reflection on the Government. If People should not be called to account for possessing the People with an ill Opinion of the Government, no Government can subsist, For it is very necessary for all Governments that the People should have a good Opinion of it. And nothing can be worse to any Government, than to endeavour to procure Animosities; as to the Management of it, this has been always look'd upon as a Crime, and no Government can be safe without it be punished.

Now you are to consider, whether these Words I have read to you, do not tend to beget an ill Opinion of the Administration of the Government? To tell us, that those that are employed know nothing of the Matter, and those that do know are not employed. Men are not adapted to Offices, but Offices, to Men, out of a particular Regard to their Interest, and not to their Fitness for the Places; this is the Purport of these Papers.

[90] Ch. J. *Holt* in *Tutchin's* Case. [Zenger]

MR. HAMILTON. I humbly beg Your Honours Pardon: I am very much misapprehended, if you suppose what I said was so designed. Sir, you know; I made an Apology for the Freedom I found my self under a Necessity of using upon this Occasion. I said, there was Nothing personal designed; it arose from the Nature of our Defence.

The Jury withdrew and in a small Time returned and being asked by the Clerk whether they were agreed of their Verdict, and whether *John Peter Zenger* was guilty of Printing and Publishing the Libels in the Information mentioned? They answered by *Thomas Hunt*, their Foreman, *Not Guilty*, Upon which there were three Huzzas in the Hall, which was crowded with People and the next Day I was discharged from my Imprisonment.

Honoring Hamilton

In the appendix to the Narrative, *Zenger published a resolution of the New York City Council honoring Andrew Hamilton. The members of the council also voted to present Hamilton with a gold box in recognition of his "remarkable Service . . . to the Inhabitants of this City and Colony." What is the significance of this passage, both in terms of what it describes and in the fact of its inclusion in Zenger's narrative?*

APPENDIX.

City of *New-York*	} *ss.*	At a Common Council, held at the City Hall of the said City, on *Tuesday* the Sixteenth Day of *September*, Anno Dom. 1735.

PRESENT.

Paul Richards Esq; Mayor.
Gerardus Stuyvesant Esq; Deputy-Mayor.
Daniel Horsmanden, Esq; Recorder.

ALDERMEN.

William Roome Esq;   *John Walter* Esq;
Stephen Bayard Esq;   *Simon Johnson* Esq;
Christopher Fell Esq;   *Johannes Burger* Esq;

ASSISTANTS.

Mr. *Johannes Waldron.*   Mr. *John Moore.*
Mr. *Charles LeRoux.*   Mr. *Ede Myer.*
Mr. *John Fred.*   *Evert Byvanck.*

Ordered, *That* Andrew Hamilton, *Esq;* of Philadelphia, *Barrister at Law, be presented with the Freedom of this Corporation; and that Alderman* Bayard, *Alderman* Johnson, *and Alderman* Fell, *be a Committee to bring in a Draught thereof,*

| City of New-York } ss. | At a Common Council, held at the City Hall of the said City on *Monday* the twenty Ninth Day of *September*, being the Feast Day of St. *Michael* the Archangel *Anno Dom.* 1735. |

PRESENT.

Paul Richards Esq; Mayor.
Daniel Horsmanden, Esq; Recorder.

ALDERMEN.

William Roome, Esq;   *John Walter,* Esq;
Stephen Bayard, Esq;   *Simon Johnson,* Esq;
Christopher Fell, Esq;   *Johannes Burger,* Esq;

ASSISTANTS.

Mr. *Johannes Waldron.*   Mr. *Charles LeRoux.*
Mr. *Henry Bogart.*   Mr. *John Fred.*
Mr. *Evert Byvank.*

Stephen Bayard, Simon Johnson *and* Christopher Fell, Esqrs. *Alderman, to whom it was referred to prepare the Draught of the Freedom of this Corporation, to be presented to* Andrew Hamilton *Esq; make their Report thereon, in the Words following* (to wit) *That they have prepared the Form of the Grant, to the said* Andrew Hamilton, *Esq; of the Freedom of the City of* New-York, *in these words* (to wit).

| City of New-York } ss. | PAUL RICHARDS Esq; the Recorder, Aldermen and Assistants of the City of *New-York*, convened in Common-Council, To all whom these Presents shall come Greeting. |

WHEREAS, Honour is the Just Reward of Virtue, and publick Benefits demand a publick Acknowledgment. We therefore, under a grateful Sense of the remarkable Service, done to the Inhabitants of this City and Colony, by *Andrew Hamilton,* Esq; of *Pennsilvania,* Barrister at Law, by his Learned and generous Defence of the Rights of Mankind, and the Liberty of the Press, in the Case of *John Peter Zenger,* lately tried on an Information exhibited in the Supream-Court of this Colony, do by these Presents, bear to the said *Andrew Hamilton* Esq; the publick Thanks of the Freemen of this Corporation for that signal Service, which he Cheerfully undertook under great Indisposition of Body, and generously performed, refusing any Fee or Reward: And in Testimony of our great Eeem[91] for his Person, and Sense of his Merit, do hereby present him with the Freedom of this Corporation. These are therefore to Certify and Declare, that the said *Andrew Hamilton* Esq; is hereby admitted, received and allowed a Freedom[92] and Citizen of the said City: To Have, Hold, Enjoy and Partake of all the Benefits, Liberties, Priviledges, Freedoms and Immunities whatsoever granted or belonging to a Freeman and Citizen of the same City. *In Testimony,* whereof the Common Council of the said City, in Common Council assembled, have caused the Seal of the said City to be hereunto affixed this Twenty Ninth Day of *September. Anno Domini One Thousand Seven Hundred and Thirty Five.*

By Order of the Common Council
William Sharpas. Clerk

And we do further Report, that sundry of the Members of this Corporation and Gentlemen of this City have voluntarily Contributed sufficient for a Gold Box of five Ounces, and a half for Inclosing the Seal of the said Freedom; Upon the Lid of which, we are of Opinion should be engraved the Arms of the City of New-York: *Witness Our Hands this Twenty Ninth day of* September, 1735.

Stephen Bayard.
Simon Johnson.
Christopher Fell.

Which Report is approved by this Court, and Ordered, *That the Freedom and Box be forthwith made, pursuant to the said Report, and that* Mr. Sharpas, *the Common Clerk of this City, do affix the Seal to the same Freedom, and inclose it in said Box.*

---

[91] So printed in the original for "Esteem." [Zenger]
[92] So given in the original for "Freeman." [Zenger]

Mr. Alderman *Bayard going to* Philadelphia *and offering to be the Bearer of the said Freedom to Mr.* Hamilton, Ordered *That* Mr. Sharpas, *deliver it to Alderman* Bayard *for that Purpose; and that Alderman* Bayard *do deliver it to Mr.* Hamilton, *with Assurances of the great Esteem, that this Corporation have for his Person and Merit.*

City of   ⎱   *ss.*   At a Common Council, held at the City
New-York ⎰   Hall of the said City, on *Wednesday* the fifteenth Day of *October*, Anno Domini 1735.

PRESENT.

Paul Richards, Esq; Mayor.
Daniel Horsemanden, Esq; Recorder.

ALDERMEN.

John Walter, Esq;   *William Roome*, Esq;
Simon Johnson, Esq;   *Johannes Burger*, Esq;

ASSISTANTS.

Mr. *Johannes Waldron*,   Mr. *Gerrardus Beekman*,
Mr. *Henry Bogart*,   Mr. *Abraham de Peyster*,
Mr. *Peter Stoutenburgh*,

Ordered, *That the Freedom, granted by this Corporation, to* Andrew Hamilton, *Esq; with the Report of the Committee, for preparing a Draught of the same and the Order of this Court, thereon, may be printed.*

William Sharpas.

Round on the Lid of the Box mentioned in the above said Report and Order, there is engraved not only the Arms of the City of *New-York*, but also this Motto in a Garter;

DEMERSÆ LEGES-TIMEFACTA LIBERTAS-HÆC
TANDEM EMERGUNT.[93]

On the inner Side of the Lid of the Box shewing it self at the same Time with the Certificate of the Freedom; There is Engraven in a flying Garter, these Words.

---

[93] "One may circumvent the laws, threaten liberty; nevertheless these will eventually rise up." This is from Cicero, *De Officiis*, 2.7.24.

NON NUMMIS, — VIRTUTE PARATUR.[94]

As an Incentive to publick Virtue, on the Front of the Rim of the said Box, there is Engraven a Part of *Tully's* Wish;

ITA CUIQUE EVENIAT, UT DE REPUBLICA MERUIT.[95]

Which Freedom and Box was presented in the Manner that had been directed, and gratefully accepted by the said *Andrew Hamilton*, Esq;

ERRATA.[96]

Pag. 12 Lin. 8. *for* Who *read* tho'. The same Page, Lin. 9 for *Freeholders* read *Freehold.* The same Page, Lin. 11. *for* be out *read* be left out. Pag. 13. Lin. *penult. for* said the *read* the said.

New-York, Printed and sold by *John Peter Zenger.*
MDCCXXXVI

---

[94]"Not by mere coins can virtue be bought." The correct Latin phrase should have been "Non nummis virtus paratur."

[95]"Thus, however things turn out, let it be merited by the republic."

[96]The mistakes listed in this Errata have been corrected in this reprinting of the *Narrative* (see pp. 69–70 and 72).

Related Documents

1

NEW YORK WEEKLY JOURNAL

An Essay on the Liberty of the Press

November 12 and 19, 1733

This anonymously written essay appeared in two parts in the second and third issues of Zenger's paper, the New York Weekly Journal. *It illustrates how Zenger and his supporters both argued for freedom of the press and used the press as a political tool to expose the corruption of the Cosby administration. The arguments here are far in advance of the state of the law in England in the early eighteenth century. They also propound a notion of a free press that is more sweeping than most people in England or America would have accepted at the time. However, by putting a free press into action, Zenger and his supporters were able to create a climate that led to greater public support for a free press.*

It is worth noting that in this essay, the author contrasts slavery with liberty. Colonial New York at this time had a considerable number of slaves, and thus the contrast was one that had some meaning to the people of the colony. A generation later, the American revolutionaries of 1765–1783 would make similar comparisons and contrasts. The classical references in the article — the use of the pen name Cato, the quotations

From *New York Weekly Journal*, nos. 2 and 3, November 12 and 19, 1733.

from Tacitus — illustrate the belief of the Morrisites and the libertarian philosophers in England that the Roman republic offered a model for a society based on liberty and good government.

Number 2, Monday, November 12, 1733

Mr. *Zenger.*

Incert the following in your next, and you'll oblige your Friend,

CATO.

Mira temporum felicitas ubi sentiri quæ velis, & quæ sentias dicere licit.
—Tacit.[1]

The Liberty of the Press is a Subject of the greatest Importance, and in which every Individual is as much concern'd as he is in any other Part of Liberty: Therefore it will not be improper to communicate to the Publick the Sentiments of a late excellent Writer upon this Point. Such is the Elegance and Perspicuity of his Writings, such the inimitable Force of his Reasoning, that it will be difficult to say any Thing new that he has not said, or not to say that much worse which he has said.

There are two Sorts of Monarchies, an absolute and a limited one. In the first, the Liberty of the Press can never be maintained, it is inconsistent with it; for what absolute Monarch would suffer any Subject to animadvert on his Actions, when it is in his Power to declare the Crime, and to nominate the Punishment? This would make it very dangerous to exercise such a Liberty. Besides the Object against which those Pens must be directed, is their Sovereign, the sole supream Magistrate; for there being no Law in those Monarchies, but the Will of the Prince, it makes it necessary for his Ministers to consult his Pleasure, before any Thing can be undertaken: He is therefore properly chargeable with the Grievances of his Subjects, and what the Minister there acts being in Obedience to the Prince, he ought not to incur the Hatred of the People; for it would be hard to impute that to him for a Crime, which is the Fruit of his Allegiance, and for refusing which he might incur the Penalties of Treason. Besides, in an absolute Monarchy, the Will of the Prince

---

[1] The quotation is from Tacitus, *Histories,* and was written sometime between 100 and 110 CE. It translates as "It is the rare fortune of these days that you may think what you like and say what you think."

bcing thc Law, a Libcrty of thc Prcss to complain of Gricvanccs would be complaining against the Law, and the Constitution, to which they have submitted, or have been obliged to submit; and therefore, in one Sense, may be said to deserve Punishment, So that under an absolute Monarchy, I say, such a Liberty is inconsistent with the Constitution, having no proper Subject in Politics, on which it might be exercis'd, and if exercis'd would incur a certain Penalty.

But in a limited Monarchy, as *England* is, our Laws are known, fixed, and established. They are the streight Rule and sure Guide to direct the King, the Ministers, and other his Subjects: And therefore an Offence against the Laws is such an Offence against the Constitution as ought to receive a proper adequate Punishment; the several Constituents of the Government, the Ministry, and all subordinate Magistrates, having their certain, known, and limited Sphere, in which they move; one part may certainly err, misbehave, and become criminal, without involving the rest, or any of them in the Crime or Punishment.

But some of these may be criminal, yet above Punishment, which surely cannot be denyed, since most Reigns have furnished us with too many Instances of powerful and wicked Ministers, some of whom by their Power have absolutely escap'd Punishment, and the Rest, who met their Fate, are likewise. Instances of this Power as much to the Purpose; for it was manifest in them, that their Power had long protected them, their Crimes having often long preceeded their much desired and deserved Punishment and Reward.

That *Might over comes Right*, or which is the same Thing, that Might preserves and defends Men from Punishment, is a Proverb established and confirmed by Time and Experience, the surest Discoverers of Truth and Certainty. It is this therefore which makes the Liberty of the Press, in a limited Monarchy, and in all its Colonies and Plantations, proper, convenient, and necessary, or indeed it is rather incorporated and interwoven with our very Constitution; for if such an over grown Criminal, or an impudent Monster in Iniquity, cannot immediately be come at by ordinary Justice, let him yet receive the Lash of Satyr, let the glaring Truths of his ill Administration, if possible, awaken his Conscience, and if he has no Conscience, Rouze his Fear, by shewing him his Deserts, sting him with the Dread of Punishment, cover him with Shame, and render his Actions odious to all honest Minds. These Methods may in Time, and by watching and exposing his Actions, make him at least more Cautious, and perhaps at last bring down the great haughty and secure Criminal, within the Reach and Grasp of ordinary Justice. This advantage therefore of Exposing the exorbitant Crimes of wicked Ministers under a limited Monarchy, makes the Liberty of the Press, not only consistent with, but a necessary Part of the Constitution it self.

It is indeed urged, that the Liberty of the Press ought to be restrained, because not only the Actions of evil Ministers may be exposed, but the Character of good ones traduced. Admit it in the strongest Light, that Calumny and Lyes would prevail, and blast the Character of a great and good Minister; yet that is a less Evil than the Advantages we reap from the Liberty of the Press, as it is a Curb, a Bridle, a Terror, a Shame, and Restraint to evil Ministers; and it may be the only Punishment, especially for a Time. But when did Calumnies and Lyes ever destroy the Character of one good Minister? Their benign Influences are known, tasted, and felt by every Body: Or if their Characters have been clouded for a Time, yet they have generally shin'd forth in greater Lustre: Truth will always prevail over Falshood.

The Facts exposed are not to be believed, because said or published; but it draws Peoples Attention, directs their View, and fixes the Eye in a proper Position, that every one may judge for himself, whether those Facts are true or not. People will recollect, enquire and search, before they condemn; and therefore very few good Ministers can be hurt by Falshood, but many wicked Ones by seasonable Truth: But however the Mischief that a few may possibly, but improbably, suffer by the Freedom of the Press, is not to be put in Competition with the Danger which the KING and the *People* may suffer by a shameful, cowardly Silence, under the Tyrany of an insolent, rapacious, infamous Minister.

Number 3, Monday, November 19, 1733

[The Remainder of the Letter, concerning the Liberty of the Press, begun in our last.]

Inconveniences are rather to be endured than that we should suffer an entire and total Destruction. Who would not lose a Leg to save his Neck? And who would not endanger his Hand to guard his Heart? The Loss of Liberty in general would soon follow the Suppression of the Liberty of the Press; for as it is an essential Branch of Liberty, so perhaps it is the best Preservative of the whole. Even a Restraint of the Press would have a fatal Influence. No Nation Antient or Modern ever lost the Liberty of freely Speaking, Writing, or Publishing their Sentiments, but forthwith lost their Liberty in general and became Slaves. *LIBEERTY* and *SLAVERY*! how amiable is one! how odious and abominable the other! Liberty is universal Redemption, Joy, and Happiness; but Servitude is absolute Reprobation and everlasting Perdition in Politics.

All the venal Suportors of wicked Ministers are aware of the great use of the Liberty of the Press, in a limited free Monarchy: They know how vain it would be to attack it openly, and therefore endeavour to puzzle the Case with Words, Inconsistencies, and Nonsense; but if the Opinion of the most numerous, unprejudiced and impartial Part of Mankind is an Argument of Truth, the Liberty of the Press has that as well as Reason on its Side. I believe every honest *Britton*, of whatever Denomination, who loves his Country, if left to his own free and unbyassed Judgment, is a Friend to the Liberty of the Press, and an Enemy to any Restraint upon it. Surely all the independent Whiggs, to a Man, are of this Opinion. By an *Independent Whigg*, I mean one whose Principles lead him to be firmly attached to the present happy Establishment, both in Church and State, and whose Fidelity to the Royal Family is so staunch and rivitted, as not to be called in Question, tho' his Mind is not over-swayed, or rather necessitated, by the extraordinary Weight of lucrative Posts or Pensions. The Dread of Infamy hath certainly been of great Use to the Cause of Virtue, and is a stronger Curb upon the Passions and Appetites of some Men, than any other Consideration Moral or Religious. Whenever, therefore, the Talent of Satyr is made use of to restrain Men, by the Fear of Shame, from immoral Actions, which either do or do not fall under the Cognizance of the Law, it is properly, and justly, and commendably applied: On·the contrary, to condemn all Satyr is in Effect the same Thing as contenancing Vice, by screening it from Reproach and the just Indignation of Mankind. The Use of Satyr was of great Service to the Patriot Whiggs in the Reign of King *Charles* and King *James* the second, as well as in that of Queen *Anne*. They asserted the Freedom of Writing against wicked Ministers; and tho' they knew it would signify nothing to accuse them publickly, whilst they were in the Zenith of their Power, they made use of Satyr to prepare the Way and alarm the People against their Designs. If Men in Power were always Men of Integrity, we might venture to trust them with the Direction of the Press, and there would be no Occasion to plead against the Restraint of it; but as they have Vices like their Fellows, so it very often happens, that the best intended and the most valuable Writings are the Objects of their Resentment, because opposite to their own Tempers or Designs. In short, I think, every Man of common Sense will judge that he is an Enemy to his King and Country who pleads for any Restraint upon the Press; but by the Press, when Nonsense, Inconsistencies, or personal Reflections are writ, if despised, they die of Course; if Truth, solid Arguments, and elegant, just Sentiments are published, they should meet with Applause rather than Censure; if Sense and Nonsense are blended, then, by the free Use of the Press, which is open to all, the Inconsistencies of the

124 RELATED DOCUMENTS

Writer may be made apparent; but to grant a Liberty only for Praise, Flattery, and Panegyric, with a Restraint on every Thing which happens to be offensive and disagreeable to those who are at any Time in Power, is absurd, servile, and rediculous; upon which, I beg Leave to quote one Observation of the ingenious Mr. *Gordon*, in his excellent Discourses upon *Tacitus*. *"In Truth,"* says he, *"where no Liberty is allowed to speak of Governours, besides that of praising them, their Praises will be little believed; their Tenderness and Aversion to have their Conduct examined, will be apt to prompt People to think their Conduct guilty or weak, to suspect their Management and Designs to be worse perhaps than they are, and to become turbulent and seditious, rather than be forced to be silent."*

2

NEW YORK WEEKLY JOURNAL

Zenger's "Criminal" Articles

December 17, 1733, and September 23, 1734

On November 6, 1734, the sheriff of New York ordered that four issues of the New York Weekly Journal—*numbers 7, 47, 48, and 49—be publicly burned. This was to comply with a request from the Governor's Council, which was dominated by supporters of Governor Cosby. The New York Assembly and the upper chamber of the New York City Council, or Court of Quarter Sessions, refused to cooperate with this suppression of the paper, so the Governor's Council ordered the New York sheriff to burn the papers, which he eventually did. The next two documents are excerpted from issues 7 and 47 and illustrate how Zenger's paper annoyed and angered Cosby. These articles move beyond theoretical arguments about free speech or sarcastic little digs aimed at Cosby or his henchmen. Instead, they attack Cosby's judgment and even his patriotism. Zenger would eventually be prosecuted on the basis of these publications.*

From *New York Weekly Journal*, no. 7, December 17, 1733, and no. 47, September 23, 1734.

An Article Questioning Cosby's Judgment in Foreign Affairs

Early in Cosby's administration, a French ship asked permission to dock in New York to purchase food for the French colony in Canada. At the time, England and France were at peace, but this peace was merely a hiatus in what was nearly a century of warfare between the two nations, including King William's War (1689–1697), Queen Anne's War (1702–1713), and, after Zenger's case, King George's War (1744–1748) and the French and Indian War (1754–1763). The Morrisites understood, as did almost all politically sophisticated people in England and the colonies, that another war with France was almost certainly just over the horizon. In this context, the willingness of Cosby to allow a French ship to dock in New York was rather shocking. As a military man, he ought to have known better. This article, which is really just a series of probing questions followed by some political statements, is a pointed attack on Cosby's judgment as a governor and military leader and implies that Cosby was at best merely incompetent and dangerous. The underlying message of the article is that Cosby was working against the best interests of the king and the British Empire.

It is agreed on all Hands, that a Fool may ask more Questions than a wise Man can answer, or perhaps will answer if he could; but notwithstanding that, I would be glad to be satisfied in the following Points of Speculation that the above Affidavits afford. And it will be no great Pussle to a wise Man to answer with a *Yea*, or a *Nay*, which is the most that will be required in most of those Questions.

Q. 1. *Is it prudent in the* French *Governours not to suffer an* English-man *to view their Fortifications, sound their Harbours, tarry in their Country to discover their Strength?*

Q. 2. *Is it prudent in an* English *Governour to suffer a* French *Man to view our Fortifications, sound our Harbours?* &c.

Q. 3. *If the above Affidavits be true, had the* French *a bad Harvest in Canada? or do they want Provisions?*

Q. 4. *Was the Leteer from the Governour of* Louisburgh *to our Governour true?*

Q. 5. *Might not our Governour as easily have discovered the falshood of it as any Body else, if he would?*

Q. 6. *Ought he not to have endeavoured to do it?*

Q. 7. *Did our Governour endeavour to do it?*

Q. 8. *Was it not known to the greatest Part of the Town, before the* Sloop Le Caesar *left* New-York, *that the* French *in the sloop* Le Caesar *had sounded and taken the Land-Marks from without* Sandyhok *up to* New-York? *Had taken the View of the Town? Had been in the Fort?*

Q. 9. *Might not the Governour have known the same Thing, if he would?*

Q. 10. *Is there not great Probability that he did know it?*

Q. 11. *Was it for our Benefit or that of the French these Soundings and Land-Marks were taken, and Views made?*

Q. 12. *Could we not, by seizing their Papers, and confining their Persons, have prevented them in great Measure from making use of the Discoveries they made?*

Q. 13. *Ought they not to have been so prevented?*

Q. 14. *Was it prudent to suffer them to pass through* Hellgate, *and also to discover that Way of Access to us?*

Q. 15. *If a* French *Governour had suffered an* English *Sloop and Company to do what a* French *Sloop and Company has done here, would he not have deserved to be——?*[2]

Q. 16. *Since it appears by the Affidavits, there was no such Scarcity of Provisions, as by the Letter from the Governour of* Louisburgh *to our Governour is set forth, since the Conduct of the* French *to the* English *that happen to go to* Canada, *shews they think it necessary to keep us ignorant of their State and Condition as much as they can. Since the Sounding our Harbours, viewing our Fortifications, and the honourable Treatment they have received here (the reverse of what we receive in* Canada) *has let them into a perfect Knowledge of our State and Condition. And since their Voyage must appear to any Man of the least Penetration to have been made with an Intent to make that Discovery, and only with that Intent. Whether it would not be reasonable in us to provide as well and as soon as we can for our Defence?*

Q. 17. *Whether that can be done any way so well and effectually as by calling the Assembly very soon together?*

---

[2] Here Zenger, for prudential reasons, does not say what *ought* to happen to a governor who acts in this manner, but the implication is that such a governor might be executed for treason.

Q. 18. *If this be not done, and any dangerous Consequences follow after so full Warning, Who is blameable?*

Sir; *Be pleased to incert in your next Paper the following List of the Honourable Gentlemen Members of the Council, usually summoned to Council by His Excellency the Governour, and you'll oblige one of your Subscribers.*

The Honourable *George Clarke*, Esq; Secratery of this Province, and, by that Office, Clerk of the Council.

The Honourable *Francis Harrison*, Esq; Judge of the Admirality of the Province of *New-York,* and *New-Jersey,* Recorder of the City of *New-York,* Examiner of the High and Honourable Court of Chancery, before His Excellency the Governour, and Surveyor and Searcher of His Majesty's Customs of the Port of *New-York.*

The Honourable *Archibald Kennedy,* Esq; His Majesty's Receiver General of the Province of *New-York,* and Collector of His Majesty's Customs for the said Province.

The Honourable *James De Lancy,* Esq; lately made Chief Justice of this Province, in the Room of *Lewis Morris,* Esq; displaced.

The Honourable *Daniel Horsmanden,* Esq; a Gentleman lately come to this Province, and more lately by His Excellency our Governour's Recommendation (as is said) appointed one of His Majesty's Council, having first been, and still he is, one of His Excellency's Council in His Suit in the King's Name against the Honourable *Rip Van Dam,* Esq;.

The Honourable *Henry Lane,* Esq; recommended and appointed as Mr. *Horsmanden.*——My Intelligence, I must own, is not so good as to be able to inform you what Office he as yet has. Besides:

Sundry others of the Gentlemen of the Council, who have no Offices, nor expect any, live also in Town; but few of them have often the Honour of being summoned to Council; and one of them, it is talkt, has not been once summoned since *November* 1732, tho' it is said, he has been in Town at the Time of every one of the Councils since: But as five do make a *Quorum,* and when five do meet, the *Majority* of them do determine the Point in Question, it would seem, that it is thought, there's no Need of those (whom we beg Leave to call) INOFFICIOUS GENTLEMEN OF THE COUNCIL, seeing enough of more *fit* Members are to be had.

The Middletown Letters

The three anonymously written "Middletown letters" that appeared in issues 47, 48, and 49 of the Weekly Journal *did not directly attack Cosby's ethics, judgment, or patriotism. They were not nasty, like some of the "advertisements" in the paper, nor were they particularly sarcastic. Stanley Katz, the great historian of Zenger, has argued that the letters were not libelous, even by the standards of the time. So, too, did Zenger's attorneys. The author of the letters, "Jeremy Anonymous, junr.," purports to be living in Middletown, New Jersey, and is writing about the politics of that colony. Cosby was the governor of New Jersey as well as New York, so the letters are about him, even if they do not specifically address his performance as governor of New York. In that sense, one might argue that if Zenger were to be tried for seditious libel on the basis of these letters, he should be tried in New Jersey. But this technical issue aside, the Middletown letters were written to undermine Cosby's credibility and his administration. This analysis reflects the assertion of England's Chief Justice John Holt in* Rex v. Tutchin *(1704) that it was illegal for publishers to print things that would cause "the people [to have] an ill opinion of the government" because "it is very necessary for all governments that the people should have a good opinion of it." Cosby wanted Zenger arrested for publishing the Middletown letters because they would lead people to have an "ill opinion" of the governor and his administration. Following are excerpts from the second Middletown letter.*

Number 47, Monday, September 23, 1734

A second Continuation of the Letter from Middletown.

Pray (says the Councellor very gravely) if a Nullity of Laws is to be inferred from the Governours voting in Council, what will become of the Support of Government? Our Governours (its said) have always done so, and believe they do so in the Neighbouring Governments of *York* and *Pensilvania*, &c. and I never heard that the Councils (whose Business it was) either there or here, ever opposed the Governour's Sitting and Acting in Council: And, Sir, do you consider the dangerous Consequence of a Nullity of Laws? The Support of Government, answered the Lawyer, is but temporary, and in a little Time will expire by its own Limitation: But were it perpetual, I can't understand how a Government is supported by breaking the Constitution of it; that seems a Contradiction in Terms, and like *Shoaring up a House by pulling of it down.* But if you mean by the Support of the Government, the Support of the Governour and of you Officers, I see no Reason why that should be at the Expence of the Constitution, and Burdens laid upon the Subject in a manner not warranted by Law; when it can be done with as much Ease the Right Way.——The Council (it is true) are more immediately concerned in

Opposing this Voting, because the Indignity is more immediatly offered to them: But why the Assembly should not be as much concerned in supporting the Constitution, and defending any Attack made upon it, I cannot see; since the People they represent are in General[.] I see the Journals of the Assembly lying there, search them, you will find an Assembly remonstrating against the mad Practices of a Governour and the vile Implements of his Oppression; upon which he was recalled. Look a little farther, and under the Administration of General *Hunter* (who was a Man as tenacious of Power and knew as well how to use it as most Men) you will find the Assembly sending their Bills up to the Council, and in particular to the President of the Council; all this he admitted, and never once attempted to dispossess the Messengers that brought them, on the Pretence that they ought to have been delivered to him: If he had; That Assembly consisting of Members who had no private left Handed Views, were not so weak and low Spirited as to suffer such an Attempt to pass without Remarking, in a Manner suitable to the Violence of such a Conduct.——You, Sir, may know (tho' I do not) what has been always done by our former Governours: Some of them have had Impudence enough to call every Opposition to their unwarrantable and extravagant Actions, and the dispicable Wretches they employed to promote their Purposes, a Resistance and Opposition of the Royal Prerogatives of the Crown: And, Sir, (with Submission) I think their Practices ought never among sober and free Men to be alledged as Presidents[1] fit to follow.——What the Governours of the neighbouring Governments of *New-York, Pensilvania,* &c. have done, I neither do, nor am concerned to know, any more than they are with what our Governours do or have done here: The Constitution of their Governments may be different from ours; and what is unlawful here, may be lawful there for ought I know. I am not concerned and meddle not with them or any of them; nor ought they or any of them to meddle with us, it is of *Jersey* I speak; and of *Jersey* I would be understood to speak; and of no other Place whatsoever. As to your Nullity of Laws, I take that to be a Sort of Bugbear, fit only to be used to freighten Children; and can be urged with equal Force had the Laws been made by any one Branch of the Legislature: And must a Man decline in such Case the saying, *they are not binding,* lest they loose their unlawful Force, and which indeed they ought to loose? The Question is not, *What are the Consequences of a Nullity of Laws?* But, *Whether they are Null or not?* And, *if made only by one, or two Branches of the Legislature when they ought to be made by three?*——The

[1] *Presidents:* precedents.

Answer is easy, and what every Man in Duty to his Country, himself, and his Posterity, ought to give.——And whatever the Consequences be in such Case, they are chargeable upon those who took upon them to do what they ought not to have done; and not upon those who legally dispute or refuse to obey an illegal Command.——Nor do I see the mighty Danger of esteeming any Laws void that really are so.——If the matter of many of them be convenient or necessary for the Comunity, tho' made by an incompetent Authority; the Nullity of them is easily and quickly remedied, by enacting such of them as are fit to be enacted, by a competent Authority: But a Breaking in and making a Nullity of the Constitution, not only infers, but introduces *a Nullity of Liberty*, which I think every Freeman is to guard against as much as he can.

A Gentleman present, who had all this Time been very attentive, said to the Lawyer, that what had been spoken with respect to the Governour's Acting and Voting in the passing of Bills in Council, and the Effect it had upon our Laws and Constitution, was intirely new to him . . . : as he seemed to be acquainted with the Nature of our *Jersey* Constitution, he desired Leave to ask him, *Why the late President[2] adjourned the Assembly of this Province by Proclamation in the King's Name, and under the Seal of the Province; since the Governours did it by Proclamation in their own Name, and (if seal'd at all) with their own private Seal?* Who replied, he could not pretend to know the Motives that induced the late President to differ from the Practice of former Governours: But if the late President could adjourn the Assembly at all, he believed he had taken the right Method of doing of it: For tho' the Governour had Power to call, prorogue, and disolve Assemblies, as he has to make Judges and Justices, yet he cannot do this in his own Name, and by his own private Seal. . . . A Proclamation to adjourn or prorogue a General Assembly in *Jersie*, is one of the highest Acts of Government here, and should be under the Seal of the Province and in the King's Name; and when a Governour issues such a Proclamation in his own Name, and under his own private Seal, the Practice of his Predecessors may perhaps be admitted for an Excuse for his Vanity, but the Law can never justify the Presumption of the practice, nor our Assembly be adjourned or prorogued by any such Proclamation.

[2]This is a reference to Lewis Morris, who was president of the New Jersey Council while also serving as chief justice of the New York Supreme Court. In 1719, Morris, as acting governor of New Jersey, had adjourned the New Jersey Assembly in the name of the king, whereas Cosby had done so in his own name, which the writer of the Middletown letters considered an illegal attempt by Cosby to increase his power and prestige.

You seemed to make a Question (said the Gentleman) *whether the late President could adjourn the Assembly, do you think he had less Power than the Governour had?*—I made that question (replied the Lawyer) not from any Doubt that I had of the President's Power, believing that to be equal with the Governour's; but from a Belief that I had, that neither the one nor the other could do it; which Belief was not founded on the Want of Power in the President (if a Governour or President could adjourn [as either could prorogue] which will admit of Debate) but from the Want of an Assembly in being to be adjourned, which I think pretty clearly appears from what has been already said: The Assembly not having been adjourn'd or prorogued by the late Governour, by any Instrument under the Seal of the Province of *New-Jersie*; and therefore no Assembly in being to be adjourned or prorogued by the President:—But I shall say something more, in order to clear this Matter farther up, if possible.——A Prorogation, if done before the Time appointed in the Writ for the Meeting of the Parliament, is a putting of the Time of Meeting the Parliament off to a farther Time; and this is done by an Instrument under the great Seal. And the Beginning of the Parliament is not the Day on which the Writs are made returnable; but the Day of their Meeting appointed by the Prorogation; *Dyer*, 203. *pl.* 72. *2d. Keb.* 820. *pl.* 30. But a Prorogation after Meeting puts a Period to the Sessions, and discontinues every Thing unfinish'd in that Sessions; which must begin (if at all) in another *de novo*. The Day of the Summons is the Beginning of that Parliament so prorogued, *Raym.* 192. I *Lev.* 296. *2d. Keb.* 820. *pl.* 30, 686. *pl.* 10. An Adjournment is made by each House, and is a Suspension of their Acting, and a Continuance of their Session, and of every Thing before them to be proceeded on at the Time to which they are adjourned. A Parliament prorogued to a Day certain, and summoned before that Day, it was agreed by the Judges that the Summons was contrary to Law, and they were again prorogued to the same Day as before, *Syderfin* 330. *pl.* 1. A Parliament adjourned to a certain Day, but the Crown intending to prorogue before that Day consulted the Judges, who agreed that they must be prorogued on the very Day to which it was adjourned, and a Proclamation was published to notify this Intention, that no more of the Members might meet than what were sufficient to make a House, I *Syderfin* 393. *pl.* 26. I shall not multiply Authorities.—An Adjournment . . . necessarily presuposes Persons met at the time of Adjournment, and that Meeting to be adjourned, and a Time certain to which it is adjourned, whether this is done by the House or by the King.—King *Charles* I (a Prince as fond of Prerogative as any) sent to the House to adjourn themselves; but the House or Sir *John Elliot*, &c.

would not suffer the Speaker to adjourn them, and Sir *John Elliot* and others were prosecuted for hindering of him and keeping of him in the Chair, and was fin'd severally for doing of it.——That the Parliament adjourn themselves, and that our Assembly adjourn themselves is known to all; and it is impossible to conceive how any Assembly of Men could adjourn themselves that were not met before they adjourned. Queen *Elizabeth* is one Instance of adjourning a Parliament, and possibly there may be some more, but if any, very few; and that of the Queen was, and the other must have been, after they were met, the very Term implying so much; and every Adjournment being a Continuance of the Proceedings then before them, must presupose that such Proceedure there was to be continued. . . .

3

NEW YORK WEEKLY JOURNAL

An *"Illegal"* Attack on the Attorney General

January 28, 1734

When Attorney General Richard Bradley brought charges against Zenger in January 1735, he referred to issues 13 and 23 of the New York Weekly Journal, *asserting that articles appearing in those issues libeled the governor. The main argument of the following essay from issue 13 is that the administration, including Attorney General Bradley, was threatening the liberty of the press and might impose slavery on New Yorkers by denying them their fundamental liberties. Nothing in the article is direct, an example of how Zenger's press struck at the governor through innuendo rather than by name. But like the Middletown letters, this brief essay was clearly designed to undermine confidence in the governor and the attorney general, and that technically might have been a libel.*

From *New York Weekly Journal*, no. 13, January 28, 1734.

Domestic Affairs.

To the Authors of the Letter to Mr. Bradford, *in his Gazette of* January 21, 1733–4.[1]

Gentlemen;
Your Apearance in Print at last, gives a Pleasure to many, tho' most wish that you had come fairly into the open Field, and not appeared behind Retrenchments made of the SUPPOSED *Laws against Libelling,* and of, what other Men have said and done before: These Retrenchments, *Gentlemen,* may soon be shewn to you and all Men to be weak, and, have neither Law nor Reason for their Foundation, so cannot long stand you in stead. Therefore you had much better as yet leave them, and come to what THE PEOPLE of this City and Province think are the Points in Question, *to witt*:

They think, as Matters now stand, that their LIBERTIES *and* PROPERTIES *are precarious, and that* SLAVERY *is like to be entailed on them and their Posterity, if some past Things be not amended. And this they collect from many past Proceedings.*

You Gentlemen think, that Things past are right, and that Things may go on in the same Way, without such Consequence.

These Points, Gentlemen, highly concern the PEOPLE of this Province, and you as well as the rest; it is your Interest as well as theirs to have them fairly searched into, by Inquiry into Facts, and by plain and fair Arguments upon them without Passion. If you are right in your Thoughts, then there will be no Harm by or from the fair and thorough Inquiry: But should you be wrong, and the Consequence dreaded follow, for want of a timely Inquiry and Remedy, your Posterity as well as ours will be Sufferers; nay, you have most Reason to fear, that your Posterity will be the first that will fall by establishing UNBRIDLED POWER.

As the Liberty of the press is now struck at, which is the Safeguard of all our other Liberties: This starts another Point worth Discussing, which by many was thought, would never have needed to have been handled here more than it has been: And undoubtedly it is one of the first Things that ought to be examined into fairly before the World.

What other Men have said and done (unless right) can be no Justification for following their Example; These Men ought, and we believe soon will, severally justify what they have said and done, or confess wherein they have erred, and make all reasonable Satisfaction for their Errors.

[1] The date here reflects an old calendar system in which March, not January, was the first month of the year. Under a modern calendar, the date of the issue of the *Gazette* referenced here would in fact be January 21, 1734.

If any Thing has been too stinging in what has been printed here, it is believed, your delaying so long in coming to the Press, in order to a fair Inquiry, was the Cause, and will excuse it.

These are the Sentiments of many of this City and Province, and it is hoped that Passions of neither Side will draw the Disputants off from the Points in Question.

4

ANGLO-AMERICANUS

Response to the Zenger Narrative

July 20, 1737

The Zenger case was a landmark for those who wanted a world where, in the words of Tacitus, you were free to "think what you like and say what you think" (see Document 1). But for supporters of the status quo, Zenger's case represented a dangerous societal change: The Zenger verdict was surely a result of jury nullification—a case where, contrary to the facts and the law, a runaway jury acquitted a guilty man. Those who revered the majesty of the law worried that if other juries followed this example, the law would have no meaning and society would be threatened by persistent lawlessness. It was hardly a stretch of the imagination to believe that if publishers could be acquitted because the jury liked their politics, rioters and even murderers might also be acquitted of their crimes. Conservatives also saw the case as an example of an otherwise venerable lawyer, Andrew Hamilton, urging a jury to disobey the law. The consequences of such behavior would be profoundly dangerous to society, as lawyers were responsible for supporting an ordered society, not disrupting it. Conservatives were not against liberty, but they believed that liberty could be made secure only through a law-abiding society. Liberty mattered only if there was security and order. Zenger's case threatened all this.

From Anglo-Americanus [Jonathan Blenman], *Remarks on Zenger's Tryal, Taken out of the Barbados Gazette's. For the Benefit of the Students in Law, and Others in North America* (Philadelphia: Andrew Bradford, 1737).

Not surprisingly, a few conservative supporters of existing legal rules and orderly society attacked the Zenger verdict and Zenger's Narrative. *The most persuasive critic was Jonathan Blenman, the attorney general (his title was "king's attorney") in the colony of Barbados. Writing under the pseudonym Anglo-Americanus, Blenman composed a long critique of Hamilton's arguments in the Zenger trial. Blenman's essay first appeared in the* Barbados Gazette *on July 20, 1737, and was later reprinted in New York by William Bradford (Cosby's official printer) and in Philadelphia by William Bradford's son, Andrew Bradford. The essay, excerpted here, is lawyerly and scholarly, making the case for an orderly society in which governors are not openly criticized and thus are able to do their job. Anglo-Americanus's essay may have been persuasive to the elite planter class in Barbados; the colony had a huge slave majority, and the minority white population lived in constant fear of slave disorder and rebellion and fully understood the dangers that could arise from unbridled free speech. His arguments were less persuasive to the majority of New Yorkers, however, who saw their own liberty threatened by governors such as Cosby and by the legal theories of men such as Blenman.*

This Lawyer seems to be above having his Points of Law decided by Authorites of the Law; and has something in Reserve, which may serve to overthrow not only what has been offer'd in this Paper, but even all the Books of the Law. This is what he calls *the Reason of the thing*, but is truly and properly a Sketch of his own *Politicks*; which leads me to shew that *the true Reason of the thing* here, agrees with the *Law* and consequently both these are against this expert Master of Law and Reason.

The *Reason of the Thing*, as well as it can be collected from a Heap of Particulars huddled together without Order and Method, may be reduced to the three following Heads.

1. The Form of an Information for Libel, and the Necessity of knowing the Truth or Falshood of its Contents, in order to direct the Judges in awarding arbitrary Punishment.

2. The Right every Man hath of publishing his Complaints, when the Matters so published can be supported with Truth.

3. The Necessity there is of using this Right, in the Plantations especially, by Reason of the Difficulty of obtaining Redress against evil Governours by any other Means.

1. . . . The Barrister throws in a shrewd Question, arising from the Form of the Information, which charges the Libel to be *false. This Word FALSE*, says he, *must have some Meaning, else how came it there? I hope Mr. Attorney will not say he put it there by Chance; and I am of Opinion his Information would not be good without it.*[1] By way of Answer to this, I must take leave to put a Question or two in the same Strain. Suppose a Man brings an Action of *Trespass*, for violating his Wife, and he fairly sets forth the Truth of the Case, *viz.* That the Defendant, *by amorous Addresses, Letters, Presents*, &c. did gain the Consent of the Plaintiff's Wife, and at length debauched her. I would ask, whether an Action of *Trespass* thus laid can be supported? I fancy not; and yet this is a more just Account of the Matter, than when *vi & armes*, viz. *swords, staves, knives*, &c. are introduced as Instruments of invading this tender Part of our Neighbours Property. Suppose further, a Man kills another whom he never saw or heard of before; and he is accused of Murdering him *of his Malice fore thought.* How come such Words to be put into an Indictment for a Fact so circumstanc'd? they must have some meaning; surely they are not put there by Chance; and I am of Opinion the Indictment would not be good without them. Why, there is this short Answer to be given to all these Childish Questions. There are many Words used in Pleadings of most kinds, sometimes for Aggravation, sometimes for Comprehension, often in Compliance with Ancient Usage, which are not traversable, and many Times are incapable of Proof. The Form of Indictments and Informations follows the Nature of the Fact, and sets it out in its worst Dress; and if the Fact is made appear to be unlawful, all the hard Names are supply'd by Implication of Law.

This is not all, quoth the Councellor; *it is said that Truth makes a Libel the more provoking; well, let us agree for once that Truth is a greater Sin than Falshood; yet as the Offences are not equal, and as the Punishment is arbitrary; is it not absolutely necessary that they should know whether the Libel is true or false, that they may by that means be able to proportion the Punishment; for would it not be a sad Case, if the Judges, for Want of a due Information, should chance to give as severe a Judgement against a Man for writing or publishing a Lie, as for writing or publishing a Truth?*[2] Now is it not a sad Case that he should want to be told, that Humans Laws don't strictly regard the moral Pravity of Actions, but their Tendency to hurt the Community, whose Peace & Safety are their principal Objects; so that by this Standard only are Punishments measur'd. If this

[1] Zeng. *Trial*, p. 82. [The citations to the *Brief Narrative* in this excerpt have been updated to reflect the pagination of this edition of the *Narrative*.]
[2] Pages 84–85.

profound Sophister is of another Opinion, let him give a Reason why it should be a greater Crime in our Law for a Man to Counterfeit a silver Shilling than to cut his Father's Throat.

2. The Right of remonstrating or publishing just Complaints, the Barrister thinks the Right of all Freemen: and so think I, provided such Remonstrances and Complaints are made in a lawful way. But when he comes to explain, it is not a Court of Justice, it is not an House of Representatives, it is not a Legislature that is to be troubled (as he phrases it) with these Things. Who then I pray, is to be troubled with them; for *the King* it seems is out of the Question? let the Barrister speak for himself; *they have a Right* (says he) *publickly to remonstrate the Abuses of Power, in the strongest Terms, to put their Neighbours upon their Guard,* &c.[3] and in another Place he speaks of it as a Hardship, *if a Man must be taken up as a Libeller, for telling his Sufferings to his Neighbour.* Now tho' I wish and hope, as earnestly as he can do, that a free People may never want the Means of uttering their just Complaints, and of redressing their Wrongs too when their Complaints are not heard; yet I always thought these Things were better understood than express'd in a Court of Law; and I shall probably remain in that Opinion till the learned Gentleman can produce something from the *Common* or *Statute Law*, to shew that a Brithish Subject has a Right of appealing publickly *to his Neighbours* (that is, to the Collective Body of the People) when he is injur'd in his Person, Rights, or Possessions. When I am assur'd that he can do this, I promise him I shall not grudge a Voyage to that Country, *where Liberty is so well understood and so freely enjoyed,*[4] that I may receive the important Discovery from his own instructive Mouth.

I know the Law Books assert the Right of Complaining to the *Magistrates and Courts of Justice,* the *Parliament,* to the *King* himself; but a Right of complaining to the *Neighbours* is what has not occurr'd to me. After all, I would not be thought to derogate, by any thing I have said or shall say, from that noble Priviledge of a free People, *the Liberty of the Press.* I think it the Bulwark of all other Liberty, and the surest Defence against Tyrany and Oppression. But still it is a Two-edged Weapon, capable of cutting both Ways, and is not therefore to be trusted in the Hands of every Discontented Fool or Designing Knave. Men of Sense and Address (who alone deserve publick Attention) will ever be able to convey proper Ideas to the People, in a Time of Danger, without runing counter to all Order and Decency, or crying *Fire* and *Murder*

[3]Page 94.
[4]Page 111.

thro' the Streets, if they chance to awake from a frightful Dream. But I
must again urge, that these Points are not fit to be discuss'd in a Court
of Justice, whose Jurisdiction is circumscribed by positive and known
Laws. Besides, they take Place properly in a Sovereign State which
has no superiour on Earth; and where an injured People can expect no
Relief but from an Appeal to Heaven. This is far from being the Case of
Colonies; and therefore I come to shew, under the third Head, that the
Barrister's *Reason of the thing* is no other than *Reason Inverted*, which
possibly may help the Project of a *Demagogue* in *America*, but can never
be reconcil'd to the Sentiments of a Lawyer, or the Principles of a Patriot,
consider'd as a Subject of *Great-Britain*.

3. I have hitherto been taught to believe that when a brave and free
People have resorted to Measures unauthoris'd by the ordinary Course
of the Laws; such Measures have been justified by the extraordinary
Necessity of the Case, which excluded all other Means of Redress, And
as far as I understand the Constitution, and have heard Accounts of the
British Colonies, such a Case cannot well happen, and has never yet
happen'd among them. But here the Barrister is ready to ask, how must
we behave when we are oppress'd by a Governour, in a Country where
the Courts of Law are said to have no coercive Power over his Person,
and where the Representatives of the People are, by his Intrigues, made
Accomplices of his Iniquity? certainly it can't be a new Discovery to tell
this Lawyer; that as the Governour is a Creature of the *Crown*; so the
most natural and easy Course is to look up to the Hand that made him.
And I imagine it may be affirm'd (without catching an Occasion of offering Incense to *Majesty*) that if one half of the Facts contain'd in *Zenger*'s
Papers and vouched for true by his Council, had been fairly represented
and proved at home, Mr. *Cosby* would not have continued much longer
in his Government; and then the City of *New-York* might have applied to
it self the Inscription of the Gold-Box; *demersæ leges, timefecta libertas,
hæc tandem emergunt;*[5] with greater propriety and security, than could
possibly be derived from the impetuous Harrangue of any Lawyer whatsoever, I am the more embolden'd to say thus much, because tho' it is
my Lot to dwell in a Colony where *Liberty has not always been well understood, at least not freely enjoy'd,* yet I have known a Governour brought
to Justice within these last Twenty Years, who was not only supported
by a Council and Assembly, besides a numerous Party here, but also
by Powerful Friends at home; all which Advantages were not able to

[5]Page 116.

screen him from Censure, Disgrace, and a Removal from the Trust he had abused. . . .

But the wild Inconsistency that shines through most Parts of this Orator's Speech, is peculiarly glaring in that Part of it now before me.[6] The Remedy which he says our Constitution prescribes for curing or preventing the Diseases of an evil Administration in the Colonies, I shall give in his own Words; *has it not been often seen (and I hope it will always be seen) that when the Representatives of a free People are, by just Representations or Remonstrances, made sensible of the Sufferings of their fellow-subjects, by the Abuse of Power in the Hands of a Governour, they have declared (and loudly too) that they were not obliged by any Law to support a Governour who goes about to destroy a Province or Colony, &c.* One would imagine, at first Sight, that this Man had the same Notion, with the Rest of Mankind, of just Representations and Remonstrances to the Representatives of a free People, which has ever been understood to be by Way of Petition or Address directed and presented to them in Form; in which Case it is hoped that they, being moved by the Complaints of the People will stretch forth their Arms to help them. But alas! we are all mistaken; for he tells us, in the same Breath, that the right Way is by telling our Sufferings to our Neighbours in Gazettes and News-Papers;[7] for the Representatives are not to be troubled with every Injury done by a Governour; besides they are sometimes in the Plot with the Governour, and the injured Party can have no Redress from their Hand; so that the first Complaint (instead of the last Resort) must be to the *Neighbours*, and so come about to the Representatives through that Channel.

Now I would be very glad to know, what the *Neighbours* can do towards effecting the desired Reformation, that will be attended with so good Success and so few ill Consequences, as a regular Application to his Majesty would be. It would be pleasant, doubtless, to hear this Politician speak out, and explain himself at large, upon this Subject. I confess it surpasses my Comprehension to conceive what the *Neighbours* inspired with weekly Revelations from the City Journalist, can do with their Governour or Assembly, unless it be to reform them by those persuasive Arguments which the *Major vis* never wants good Store of. If this be the *Patriots* meaning his Words may possibly be understood; but without this meaning, they are meer *Jargon*.

In a word; I shall agree with the Barrister (and so take my Leave of him) that *the Liberty both of exposing and opposing arbitrary Power,* is

[6]Page 93.
[7]Pages 93–94.

the Right of a free People;[8] and he ought at the same time to admit that the order of things and the Peace of Society require that extraordinary Means should not be used, for this Purpose, till the ordinary have failed in the Experiment. The supreme Magistrate of an *independant Kingdom or State*, cannot always be controul'd by the one, and then the other is justified by that Consideration. But in *Colonies*, that are from their Creation subordinate to the Mother-Country, there is no Person who is not controulable by regular and well known Methods of proceeding; and consequently there can be no absolute Necessity of flying to Extremities, at least in the first instance. From all which, I conceive, it follows, that *local considerations* upon which the Gentleman lays so great Stress, conclude directly against him; and I hope the Security which the *British* Constitution affords to every Mans Person, Property, and Reputation, as well as to the publick Tranquility, is not lessen'd by any Distance from the Fountain of Power and Justice; but that a *Libel* is a *Libel*, and punishable as such in *America* as well as in *Europe*.

[8]Page 111.

A Chronology of Events Related to the Case and Trial of John Peter Zenger (1606–1801)

1606   Court of Star Chamber in England decides the case *De Libellis Famosis*, holding that a libel can be true or false.

1624   Dutch establish the settlement of New Netherland.

1640   Long Parliament convenes.

1641   Parliament abolishes the Court of Star Chamber.

1642–1651   English Civil War.

1664   British seize New Netherland.

1688   *Trial of the Seven Bishops* in England, in which the jury refuses to convict the bishops of libeling the king, concluding that they did not author the allegedly libelous petition to the king.

1688–1689   England's Glorious Revolution.

1697   John Peter Zenger born in the German Palatinate.

1710   Zenger moves to New York with his family and is apprenticed to printer William Bradford.

1718   Zenger's apprenticeship ends, and he moves to Philadelphia.

1723   Zenger returns to New York.

1726   Zenger opens his own business after a brief partnership with Bradford.

1731   William Cosby appointed governor of New York.

1732   *August 1* Governor Cosby arrives in New York.

Zenger begins publishing anti-Cosby pamphlets and other items for Lewis Morris and James Alexander.

1733   *February* Governor Cosby asks the New York Supreme Court to sit as a court of exchequer in his suit against Rip Van Dam.

March   Chief Justice Lewis Morris dismisses Cosby's suit, ruling that the supreme court cannot sit as an exchequer court.

August   Governor Cosby removes Morris as chief justice and appoints James De Lancey to replace him.

November 5   Zenger publishes the first issue of the *New York Weekly Journal.*

1734   *January*   Grand jury refuses to indict Zenger on charges of seditious libel.

October   Another grand jury fails to indict Zenger for libel.

November 2   Governor's Council orders sheriff of New York to burn several issues of the *Weekly Journal.*

November 17   Zenger arrested.

1735   *January 28*   Attorney General Richard Bradley files an "information" charging Zenger with seditious libel.

April 16   Chief Justice De Lancey disbars James Alexander and William Smith for challenging the validity of his commission.

August 4   Zenger's trial.

August 5   Zenger released from jail.

1736   *Brief Narrative* published for the first time.

March 10   Governor Cosby dies.

1737   Zenger appointed official printer for the colony of New York; Anglo-Americanus attacks Zenger verdict in the *Barbados Gazette.*

1738   Lewis Morris becomes royal governor of New Jersey; first London reprint of *Brief Narrative.*

Zenger appointed official printer for the colony of New Jersey; *Brief Narrative* reprinted in Boston.

1741   *August 4*   Andrew Hamilton dies.

1746   *May 21*   Lewis Morris dies.

July 28   John Peter Zenger dies.

1750   *Brief Narrative* reprinted in England.

1752   *Brief Narrative* reprinted in England; William Owen tried for seditious libel.

1754–1763   French and Indian War.

1756   *Brief Narrative* reprinted in America.

April 2   James Alexander dies.

1765   *Brief Narrative* reprinted in England by John Almon.

1770 *Brief Narrative* reprinted by patriot printer John Holt.

1775 American Revolution begins.

1776 Declaration of Independence.

1784 *Brief Narrative* reprinted in England.

1787 U.S. Constitution written.

1791 Bill of Rights ratified.

1792 Britain passes Fox's Libel Act, which allows truth as a defense in libel cases and allows juries to decide the entire matter, including whether a publication is libelous.

1798 Congress passes the Sedition Act, which upholds the Zenger principle of truth as a defense and allows juries to issue general verdicts. However, the act leads to numerous trials and a dozen or so convictions of opponents of President John Adams. Most of the convictions are for opinions rather than for factual statements that can be declared true or false.

1799 *Brief Narrative* reprinted in the United States.

1801 Sedition Act expires.

Questions for Consideration

1. Why should "truth" be a defense of speech that undermines the ability of the government to operate smoothly and efficiently?
2. The English standard for libel at the time of the Zenger trial rejected truth as a defense and in fact assumed "the greater the truth, the greater the libel." Why would English judges think that people should be punished for writing something uncomplimentary about the government, regardless of whether (or especially if) what they wrote was true?
3. Were English judges and legal theorists correct in their belief that an unflattering but truthful statement about the government was more dangerous to the stability of society than an untruthful statement? Compare Andrew Hamilton's arguments on this issue during the Zenger trial with those of Anglo-Americanus in Document 4.
4. Zenger's attorneys demanded that truth should be a defense against a prosecution for criticism of the government. Is that a legitimate standard in the modern world? What if a newspaper or television reporter is "mistaken" in reporting government misconduct?
5. Andrew Hamilton argued that a jury should determine whether a publication is libelous. If you were a reporter on trial for criticizing the government, would you want to rely on a jury to protect your right to freedom of the press?
6. What do you think ought to be the modern standard for permissible criticism of the government?
7. From your reading of the *Narrative*, was Zenger misused by his wealthy patrons? Should Lewis Morris have bailed Zenger out of jail?
8. In the 1730s, New York was a small colony far from England. The royal government could not constantly or easily monitor the behavior of its colonial governors, such as Cosby. Did this make free speech and a free press more important in New York than in England? When thinking about this question, consider the argument of Anglo-Americanus that "extraordinary means" should not be used to expose government wrongdoing when "ordinary" means will do (Document 4). Andrew Hamilton, however, argued that New York was so different and so far removed from England that "ordinary means" might not work.

9. In the 1730s, New York was a small colony far from England. To the north was New France, under the control of England's perpetual enemy. To the west (and in the northern part of the colony) were untold Indians, many of them deeply hostile to English settlement in the New World. Under such circumstances, should free speech have been more restricted in New York than in England? Or should free speech have been less restricted in New York so that colonists would be able to criticize a corrupt or incompetent governor, as was done in Document 2?

10. In Document 4, Anglo-Americanus, the pen name of Jonathan Blenman, argues for stability and the importance of removing tensions between the people and the government. Blenman lived in Barbados, a British colony with a huge slave majority. Did such arguments make more sense there than in New York?

11. What are some of the principles found in the U.S. Constitution and the Bill of Rights that can be traced to the Zenger controversy?

12. The *Narrative* is written from the perspective of John Peter Zenger. The arguments of Attorney General Richard Bradley are not presented in much depth. James Alexander, who actually wrote the *Narrative*, was able to work from Andrew Hamilton's notes on the trial, but he could not (or did not) obtain such notes from Bradley. How might the *Narrative* have been different if Bradley's trial notes had been available to Alexander? Would the integration of Bradley's notes into the *Narrative* have undermined its purpose, or might it have strengthened the impact of the *Narrative* by showing just how powerful Hamilton's arguments were?

Selected Bibliography

Bailyn, Bernard. *The Ideological Origins of the American Revolution.* Cambridge, Mass.: Harvard University Press, 1967.

Benton, Laura. *Law and Colonial Cultures: Legal Regimes in World History.* New York: Cambridge University Press, 1998.

Bilder, Mary Sarah. *The Transatlantic Constitution: Colonial Legal Culture and the Empire.* Cambridge, Mass.: Harvard University Press, 2004.

Bonomi, Patricia U. *A Factious People: Politics and Society in Colonial New York.* New York: Columbia University Press, 1971.

Botein, Stephen. *"Mr. Zenger's Malice and Falsehood": Six Issues of the New-York Weekly Journal, 1733–34.* Worcester, Mass.: American Antiquarian Society, 1985.

Boxer, C. R. *The Dutch Seaborne Empire, 1600–1800.* New York: Alfred A. Knopf, 1965.

Buranelli, Vincent. "Governor Cosby and His Enemies." *New York History* 37 (1956): 565–87.

———. *The Trial of Peter Zenger.* New York: New York University Press, 1957.

Clark, Charles E. *The Public Prints: The Newspaper in Anglo-American Culture, 1665–1740.* New York: Oxford University Press, 1994.

Curtis, Michael Kent. *Free Speech, "The People's Darling Privilege": Struggles for Freedom of Expression in American History.* Durham, N.C.: Duke University Press, 2000.

Finkelman, Paul. "Zenger's Case: Prototype of a Political Trial." In *American Political Trials*, edited by Michal R. Belknap, 25–44. Rev. ed. Westport, Conn.: Greenwood Press, 1994.

Greenberg, Douglas. *Crime in the Colony of New York.* Ithaca, N.Y.: Cornell University Press, 1978.

Jacobson, David L., ed. *The English Libertarian Heritage: From the Writings of John Trenchard and Thomas Gordon in* The Independent Whig *and* Cato's Letters. Indianapolis: Bobbs-Merrill, 1965.

Kammen, Michael. *Colonial New York: A History.* New York: Scribner's, 1975.

Katz, Stanley N., ed. *A Brief Narrative of the Case and Trial of John Peter Zenger: Printer of the* New York Weekly Journal, *by James Alexander.* 2nd ed. Cambridge, Mass.: Harvard University Press, 1972.

———. *Newcastle's New York: Anglo-American Politics, 1732–1753*. Cambridge, Mass.: Harvard University Press, 1968.

———. "The Politics of Law in Colonial America: Controversies over Chancery Courts and Equity Law in the Eighteenth Century." *Perspectives in American History* 5 (1971): 257–84.

Kemmerer, Donald L. *Path to Freedom: The Struggle for Self-Government in Colonial New Jersey, 1703–1776*. Princeton, N.J.: Princeton University Press, 1940.

Launitz-Schurer, Leopold. *Loyal Whigs and Revolutionaries: The Making of the Revolution in New York, 1765–1776*. New York: New York University Press, 1980.

Leder, Lawrence H. *Liberty and Authority: Early American Political Ideology, 1689–1763*. Chicago: Quadrangle Press, 1968.

Lepore, Jill. *New York Burning: Liberty, Slavery, and Conspiracy in Eighteenth-Century Manhattan*. New York: Alfred A. Knopf, 2005.

Levy, Leonard W. "Did the Zenger Case Really Matter? Freedom of the Press in Colonial New York." *William and Mary Quarterly*, 3rd ser., 17 (1960): 35–60.

———. *The Emergence of a Free Press*. New York: Oxford University Press, 1985.

———. *Legacy of Suppression: Freedom of Speech and the Press in Early America*. Cambridge, Mass.: Harvard University Press, 1960.

———. *Origins of the Fifth Amendment: The Right against Self-Incrimination*. New York: Oxford University Press, 1968.

Mann, Bruce, and Christopher Tomlins. *The Many Legalities of Early America*. Chapel Hill: University of North Carolina Press, 2001.

Moglen, Eben. "Considering *Zenger*: Partisan Politics and the Legal Profession in Provincial New York." *Columbia Law Review* 94 (June 1994): 1495–1524.

Nash, Gary. *The Urban Crucible: The Northern Seaports and the Origins of the American Revolution*. Cambridge, Mass.: Harvard University Press, 1986.

Rutherfurd, Livingston. *John Peter Zenger: His Press, His Trial and a Bibliography of Zenger Imprints*. New York: Dodd, Mead, 1904.

Sheridan, Eugene R. *Lewis Morris, 1671–1746: A Study in Early American Politics*. Syracuse, N.Y.: Syracuse University Press, 1981.

Shorto, Russell. *The Island at the Center of the World: The Epic Story of Dutch Manhattan and the Forgotten Colony That Shaped America*. New York: Doubleday, 2004.

Siebert, Frederic S. *Freedom of the Press in England, 1476–1776: The Rise and Decline of Government Control*. Urbana: University of Illinois Press, 1952.

Smith, Jeffrey A. *Printers and Press Freedom: The Ideology of Early American Journalism*. New York: Oxford University Press, 1988.

Smith, Joseph, and Leo Hershkowitz. "Courts of Equity in the Province of New York: The Cosby Controversy, 1732–1736." *American Journal of Legal History* 16 (1972): 1–50.

Smith, William, Jr. *The History of the Province of New-York by William Smith, Jr.* Edited by Michael Kammen. 2 vols. Cambridge, Mass.: Harvard University Press, 1972.

Urofsky, Melvin, and Paul Finkelman. *A March of Liberty: A Constitutional History of the United States.* 2 vols. New York: Oxford University Press, 2002.

Warner, Michael. *The Letters of the Republic: Publication and the Public Sphere in Eighteenth-Century America.* Cambridge, Mass.: Harvard University Press, 1990.

Index